The 401(k)
MILLIONAIRE

The 401(k)
MILLIONAIRE

How I Started with Nothing and Made a Million—and You Can, Too

Knute Iwaszko

and
Brian O'Connell

Villard • New York

To Pat

Money can't buy what money can't buy

I would like to acknowledge all the people who helped to make this dream a reality: Brian O'Connell, Karen Watts, Richard Panizza, Jim Bovaso, Beth Piskora, Helen McCaffrey, Jennifer Houle.
You can see far by standing on the shoulders of giants.

Copyright © 1999 by Knute Iwaszko and Lark Productions

All rights reserved under International and Pan-American Copyright Conventions. Published in the United States by Villard Books, a division of Random House, Inc., New York, and simultaneously in Canada by Random House of Canada Limited, Toronto.

VILLARD BOOKS is a registered trademark of Random House, Inc.

Iwaszko, Knute.
    The 401(k) millionaire: how I started with nothing and made a million—and you can, too / Knute Iwaszko and Brian O'Connell.
        p.   cm.
    ISBN 978-0-812-99186-4
    1. Finance, Personal.   2. Retirement—United States—Planning.
3. 401(k) plans.   4. Investments.   I. O'Connell, Brian.
II. Title.
HG179.I96   1999
332.024′01—dc21   98-33311

Random House website address: www.atrandom.com

Printed in the United States of America on acid-free paper

A LARK PRODUCTION
BVG 01
146484122

Contents

Introduction: Where Wall Street Meets Main Street

There was a time not too long ago when only the billionaires and bare-knuckled traders ruled Wall Street. The closest average Americans got to the stock market was watching Walter Cronkite note the Dow Jones averages at the end of the *CBS Evening News*. Of course, there was also a time when I could run a marathon and had a 32-inch waist . . . but not anymore.

With the advent of the 401(k) plan in 1980, the fortunes of Wall Street and Main Street converged. The hard hat worker on a construction site now can have as much riding on the stock market as the pinstriper who occupies a plush office in a skyscraper down the block. Unfortunately, chances are that the boardroom baron might know a bit more about the intricacies of investing than the hard-hat who spends his days working with a power driver instead of a pie chart.

That's where I come in. Closing that knowledge gap and making a millionaire out of you through your 401(k) plan is my mission. It's also something I know a little bit about. No, I'm not a Wall Street whiz kid—I've worked all my life, mostly for somebody else. I've worked at everything from shining shoes to running a bed-and-breakfast inn. But I became a millionaire using my 401(k) plan and, as a result, was able to realize a dream and retire early.

How'd I do it? By applying a few simple rules to my financial behavior that ensured I made the most of my 401(k) investments. In this book, you'll hear a lot about these rules; starting early, maximizing your money, learning the ropes, understanding risk, and never, *ever* touching your 401(k) money until retirement. If you take away nothing from this book—and I think you'll take away lots—learn and live these simple rules and you, too, can retire a millionaire.

A lot of people tell me that, rules or no rules, they'll never become wealthy because they don't make enough money. Nonsense. Whether you're a school teacher or bus driver, a comfortable, secure financial future is within your grasp. Anyone can do it and I'm living proof.

I'm not saying I learned all this the easy way. I made mistakes early on and paid for them. But even though you can't change history, you can learn from it. That's what I did.

I was born and raised in Philadelphia, Pennsylvania, where I lived a normal, All-American existence growing up. Short of worrying about what it cost me to fill my car with gas, money was the furthest thing from my mind. In fact, my academic interests as a teenager leaned more toward science than anything else. With a career in science in mind, I attended Penn State University in the mid-1950s, where I studied chemistry. I graduated with a degree in chemistry and almost immediately landed a job with a Pittsburgh ceramics manufacturer. The job creating ceramic colors was unremarkable, save for two things. One, the company had no pension plan, although in the 1950s you could say that about most employers across the country. But even at a young age and with no background in finance, I knew enough to be concerned about saving money. There were certain things in life I wanted, like a house, marriage, and a family, that I knew would require some cash.

The second factor that helped shape my early opinions about money was a friend with whom I wound up sharing an apartment in order to cut down on expenses. Two bachelors with grandiose dreams, our conversations about the fortunes of the Pirates or Steelers often turned to plans of making big money in the stock market. My buddy had more experience in Wall Street matters than I did—he was one of the first mutual fund salesman in the region (Massachusetts Financial first introduced mutual funds in 1926, but they were still relatively unheard of outside Wall Street). A typical salesman, he blew a lot of smoke about the financial markets and I was never sure what to believe. But one thing he told me that has stuck to me like a barnacle on the hull of a boat is the importance of investing early. "Knute," he'd lecture me, "if you sock away $60 a month in the stock market, you'll be a millionaire by the time you reach age 65." Sixty bucks a month? That was less than what I was paying for that used MG I *had* to have when I graduated.

I immediately grasped the simple clarity of my friend's point. Just as planting seeds and carefully feeding, nurturing, and cultivating those seeds yields a lush garden, putting away a little bit of money early, cultivating it, and adding a little bit more money every year, one day you theoretically could have a million dollars. That was the seed of my dream of saving a million dollars and retiring early. It was a dream that would come true, although I never would have guessed it then.

It's a dream that can come true for you as well. If you follow my five simple rules for 401(k) investing, you can end up a 401(k) millionaire, too. Let me demonstrate how it's done.

The 401(k)
MILLIONAIRE

1

*A wise man will make many more
opportunities than he finds.*

—Francis Bacon

How I Became a
401(k) Millionaire

Back in the mid-1950s, when I was just starting out, I was a big
spender. Like many other carefree bachelors, I had to marry a good
woman before I set my priorities straight. It was time to deep-six the
bachelor mentality and create a budget so I knew where our money was
going. My wife, Pat, and I both wanted a family and a nice house, and
we knew we wanted to save for long-term goals, like college for our kids
and a nice retirement for us. I've been a runner ever since my high
school days and I still try to put in my miles. During my daily run, I'd
try to figure out how to pull some money out of our budget for investing. Keeping track of your dollars and cents is the first step to becoming a 401(k) millionaire; it's the bedrock on which everything else rests.

Once you record your monthly expenses and compare that with
your monthly pay, you can adjust your style of living accordingly. And
the earlier you do it the better. If you don't pinch pennies in the beginning, you're squandering a golden opportunity to make more money
down the road. It's what economists call "compound interest"—that's
when you earn interest not only on your original investment, but also
on the interest it has already earned. Through compounding, your investment assets grow, slowly at first, then at greater speed as the years

go by. By the time you get to the end of this book, you'll understand that compound interest is the fuel that makes your 401(k) run.

Consider a monthly investment of $300. Given a 9 percent rate of return, that $300 monthly investment turns into $22,627 after 5 years; $58,054 after 10 years, $200,366 after 20 years, and an astounding $336,337 after 25 years. In fact, the longer you leave it alone the more the interest "compounds." No wonder Albert Einstein referred to compounding as the most remarkable mathematical discovery ever! I call compound interest your very own personal money-making machine.

Back to the budget for a moment. Now, if you're thinking that Pat and I lived on oatmeal and dressed in threadbare clothes so that we could save enough to retire as millionaires, think again. We simply developed a sensible financial plan that enabled us to save money without depriving ourselves of the occasional movie or night out on the town. In fact, I don't recall being deprived of anything in those early years. All I remember is that before setting up a budget I had a hard time making it from paycheck to paycheck. After the budget kicked in, it seemed like we had extra money. Even to this day, though I can well afford it, I have never bought a new car. I'll look around for a low mileage, two-year-old car and let someone else take the depreciation. In fact, my current car is twelve years old and has rust spots, but it runs just fine. (On the other hand, though, I just bought a $500 fishing rod. You just have to learn how to keep your priorities straight!)

At first we put away only what we could each month. Another night at home instead of dining out, a few degrees lower on the oil heater, and other small household cutbacks gave us an extra $10 or $20 a month. Before long, we were putting even more away—$30, $40, and even $50 a month. Believe me, that was big money to me back in 1960.

To make the most of the extra money we were saving, I joined an investment club shortly after starting our budget. Once a month after work, I met with about six other like-minded savers who got together to take advantage of the growing attraction of the stock market. There I learned the importance of doing homework and taking responsibility for your financial future. Each month one club member would handle the research and recommend stocks to the group, who collectively gave the proposals a thumbs-up or thumbs-down. I noticed that the club members who had done their homework the best were the ones whose ideas made the most money. Thus, an avid research hound was born. To this day I read as much as I can about the financial markets, and you should, too.

At the investment club, I learned another key financial lesson: diversify. At the time, my company, Hooker Chemical, was struggling financially. The company's stock was floundering as well, and me along with it. I owned a bunch of shares myself, as did the investment club, and we all took a financial bath as the stock headed south. We'd learned that lesson the hard way, and it stayed with me the rest of my life. Always diversify your investments so that you're not too reliant on one stock, one bond, or one mutual fund. By allocating a mix of stocks, bonds, and mutual funds in your portfolio, you can minimize losses in one area and even make it up simultaneously in another area.

After I left Hooker Chemical and moved to Louisville, Kentucky, to take a job at another chemical company, my family had doubled in size so I shifted my financial plan into second gear. I shed the bad habit of being a frequent trader in favor of a buy-and-hold investment viewpoint: buying a stock or a fund and hanging onto it for a long time. As a "day-trader" (one who buys a stock in the morning and hopes to sell it the same afternoon for a profit), all I'd been doing was making my broker rich. I remember calculating that over 70 percent of the stock selections I was making at the time were money-makers. But the bottom line showed me losing money because of the sorry performance of two big stocks I held and the hefty commissions I was paying my broker for all the trades I was making. After three years, I figured I had about broken even and my broker had made $20,000 while I took all the risk. Hello, Knute? Something's wrong here! I decided I'd better quit hotdogging and learn more for myself about how the stock market really worked.

In addition to hanging on to stocks longer, I also began paying attention to things like company balance sheets and price-earnings (P/E) ratios. By spending a half-hour on the train each morning reading about the companies I was investing in, I learned to invest in the company and not the stock, another lesson that still rings true. I also adopted the Peter Lynch (the famed original portfolio manager of

Fidelity Investment's Magellan Mutual Fund, the biggest fund in the world) approach to picking companies. Lynch would walk through malls and see which stores were crowded and what products customers were buying. Taking a page out of the Lynch handbook (and then some), I'd ring up the customer service center and find out how committed the company was to satisfying customers and whether or not they stood firmly behind their product.

I also began to recognize the wisdom of investing in mutual funds and the risk of investing in individual stocks. In those years, I considered my stock investments as my potential big-ticket, home-run-type investments and my mutual funds as a savings-account-oriented afterthought. Lo and behold, my financial statements began telling an interesting story: my funds—which I never touched—were making more and more money each month while my stocks—which I traded frequently—lost me money over the years.

By the 1970s, I had left the chemical company in Louisville and switched to a career in sales. The increased demands of my new job made it more difficult to track company and industry research. Thus, I adopted an ill-advised investment strategy called "market-timing" to handle my stock investments (market timers attempt to guess the peaks and valleys of the stock market and invest accordingly). A few specialized newsletters and financial services companies claimed they could plot the timing signals for me, but you could just as easily catch a hummingbird in your hands as you could forecast the intricate patterns of the financial markets. Another lesson learned too late, as the market-timers repeatedly guessed wrong and again my investment portfolio suffered.

Fortunately, I found the silver lining in my unfortunate market-timing years that led me into the world of the 401(k). In the early 1970s, the U.S. government gave a green light to the first Individual Retirement Account (IRA), a tax-advantaged plan that enabled Americans to sock away up to $1,500 per year tax-free (that number was raised to $2,000 several years later and to $2,250 by 1998). During the stock market decline of 1973, I lost a lot of money on stocks that I would never make back again. But the mutual funds in my IRA kept my retirement portfolio on an even keel as I kept pouring money into it during good times and bad. Another lesson learned: the value of *dollar cost averaging*. More on that later.

IRAs also served another valuable purpose: they taught me the increasing value of making an investment plan and sticking to it like carpenter's glue for the long haul. For years before IRAs, my eyes would be riveted to stock listings in *The Wall Street Journal*. Stock gyrations of a couple of points or so were cause for either great satisfaction or considerable consternation in the Iwaszko household on a daily basis. Or, if I saw a mutual fund that doubled its money in a year, while mine returned only 25 percent, I'd grow very frustrated. I willingly let myself get jerked around by short-term market swings. Nobody wants to go through life like that. My IRA taught me the common-sense value of a long-term investment approach and afforded me a new—and valuable—outlook on my investments: patience.

More secure in my investment philosophy, I was now ready to embark on the last, most crucial step of my journey to becoming a 401(k) millionaire. I went to work for my last (I hope) full-time employer in 1980, just about the time the U.S. government and the IRS were approving the first 401(k) plans. I couldn't believe my ears as the human resources staffer at my new company explained their 401(k) program. In short, I was allowed to put away 6 percent of my pretax salary and my company would match half of my contribution from their own pocket. That meant if I stashed away $4,000 in my 401(k), my company was basically handing me a check for $2,000 with only one caveat: the money had to go toward my 401(k) plan. So even if my 401(k) investments made no money (and they almost always did) I was making a bushel of cash on my own, courtesy of my employer.

Even though I was out on the road a lot as a salesman I made it a point to try to research as many of the funds available to me in my 401(k) plan as I could. In the early days, that wasn't so tough. Back then there was usually a limited menu that included a stock fund, a money market fund, a bond fund, and shares in company stock. Even with fewer investment choices than the 20 or 30 fund investment options many company 401(k)s offer today, I was easily able to formulate a simple investment model to serve as the cornerstone of my 401(k) success.

Part of that plan, as I said earlier, was sticking to mutual funds, especially no-load ones that didn't charge me high fees. I liked the professional management that funds offered. I also liked the fact that fund companies were skilled marketers and placed a high premium on satisfying people like you and me. Thus, I could call the fund company 24 hours a day and get an answer if I needed one. And no-load mutual funds sell themselves. They fit a category, like growth funds or municipal bond funds, that fill your investment needs, and you can check their track record in the paper just as easily as you can look up a number in the phone book.

Mutual funds were simply the means to an end: investment vehicles that would carry my money along to retirement. Charting the course that would take me to retirement with a million dollars, however, was a different story. That required a more substantial investment model, one that I created and fine-tuned over the years and that ultimately helped make me a 401(k) millionaire. And in this book, I'm ready to share it with you.

My father, a Russian immigrant, always had to work hard for a living. Because he couldn't speak English when he first arrived in this country, he made a lot of mistakes. He taught me that it was okay to make a mistake if you never forgot its lesson. Here are the five investment lessons I learned the hard way:

Knute Says

Five Rules for Investment Success

1. *Start Early.* There is no substitute for getting a good start on your financial future. All the studies on the subject conclude that the earlier you get going with your 401(k), the more money you'll have in retirement. That's because the earlier you start, the earlier compound interest goes to work for you.

2. *Max Out.* 401(k)s provide a multitude of benefits for investors. One of the best is the plan's tax-advantaged status. In short, the more you contribute to your 401(k) plan every year, the less you'll pay in taxes to Uncle Sam. There is another advantage in maxing out and investing the legal limit in your 401(k): The more money you invest, the more your company might match, and the faster you'll become a 401(k) millionaire.

3. *Learning Is Earning.* The value of good investment research is priceless. And the value of knowing enough about your 401(k) to become the master of your financial future is just as valuable. Read all you can on finance and investments and make sure you read every word of the 401(k) packets, brochures, and memoranda that your employer sends you each year. The payoff for spending an hour or two a week boning up on the ways of Wall Street is huge, particularly as 401(k)s are expanding and going global. Don't be left behind.

4. *Be Aggressive.* Prudence is the proper course if you're an airplane pilot or a brain surgeon. But too much of it is a drawback for 401(k) investors. Studies show that to beat inflation and to make your money grow faster, a good chunk of your plan should be earmarked for higher performing stock funds. That doesn't mean you should be reckless. There's no rule that says you have to put money into Portuguese debentures because your buddy in the marketing department did. But if you stick to conservative investments like bonds or, worse, bank savings accounts, your chances of becoming a 401(k) millionaire are virtually nil.

5. *Keep the Money Working.* Over the years I participated in other profit-sharing plans. When I left those companies, I was given the option of taking the cash and rolling it over into another tax-deferred investment plan

like a 401(k) or IRA or taking the money in a lump sum and using it as I wished. The latter is a bad move and here's why: The government wants you to roll the money over and they've set up expensive traps if you don't. The IRS can take up to 20 percent of your retirement plan assets away from you if you elect to take a lump sum payout when you leave a job. If that's not grim news, consider this: They'll also tax you on the capital gains your money has earned while participating in the plan. (When you sell an investment for more than you paid, your profit is called a capital gain. It can be taxed at a rate as high as 28 percent of your earnings.) I'll cover 401(k) and IRA rollovers in Chapter 3, as well as the folly of taking loans out against your 401(k). You'll see why keeping your money working in your 401(k) isn't just your best option, it is your *only* option.

That's it. Those are my five rules for 401(k) investment success. I applied each to my own 401(k) plan early on and sat back and watched my money grow. From time to time, I'd check on my retirement portfolio, and make adjustments when I felt I needed to. But by and large, I lived by the tenets of my five rules and let the twin miracles of the stock market and compound interest take care of the rest. It would have been great if I had known how to manage my money like a pro early on, but that takes time. It really wasn't until I retired in 1994 and sat down at my kitchen table to tabulate my retirement assets that it hit me how powerfully these five rules had worked in my favor. When I saw that the final figure was well over $1 million I nearly fell out of my chair. That was a wonderful feeling and one that I want you to share. That's what this book is all about—making sure you see seven figures when you tabulate your retirement assets.

I'll go into more detail on my five rules of 401(k) investing throughout the book. I'll also spend some time discussing the wisdom of allocating your assets every year so you're investing comfortably within your risk limits and with an investment plan that makes sense for you. But first let's start by covering the basics of the 401(k) plan: how it started, its myriad benefits, and how it works.

2

The 401(k): Your Personal Money Machine

None of us wants to spend our golden years working under the golden arches. But those who rely on Social Security or who may be counting on a fat corporate pension for the bulk of their retirement assets may find themselves saying "Would you like fries with that?" forty times a day in retirement.

The good news is that a comfortable retirement will be waiting for you if you start early enough and manage your finances correctly. And the 401(k) plan is your very best chance to do just that.

The Father of the 401(k)

Imagine walking down the street one day, suddenly looking down, and finding a $100 bill. That's what a 401(k) plan is—found money. But it's money that might never have been found if it weren't for the efforts of one diligent financial planner who took an obscure reference in the mammoth Internal Revenue Service Tax Code and parlayed it into one of the biggest tax breaks in American history.

In 1980, Ted Benna was a 37-year-old retirement plan consultant in Philadelphia. Frustrated over his inability to help low- and middle-income wage earners gain the long-term financial security that he could arrange for his affluent clients, Benna was ready to hang it up and move into a new line of work.

But he made a discovery one Saturday morning in his downtown office that changed his future—and the future of millions of Americans. Pouring over the Internal Revenue Code, a favorite pastime of his, Benna uncovered a seemingly inconsequential line that enabled bank employees to participate in tax-free profit-sharing plans. The line in the Code, inserted two years earlier by IRS officials, represented a compromise between Congress and the Treasury over how to tax a profit-sharing plan.

Benna interpreted the passage to mean that for the first time ever, employees could save a good-sized chunk of their hard-earned wages in the form of pretax payroll deductions. Sensing a big idea in the making, Benna convinced his colleagues to turn his Philadelphia financial consulting firm into a guinea pig and roll out the first ever 401(k) plan to company employees. Benna hoped to attract attention, daring the IRS to try and pull the plug on a payroll-deduction plan based on a ruling from its own tax code. Thus, on January 1, 1981, the first 401(k) was born.

Despite dire warnings from financial industry naysayers, later that year the IRS upheld Benna's interpretation of the tax code and declared that employers everywhere could implement the very same retirement plan that Benna had. Four years later, with the IRS's coffers short $10 billion because of the increasingly popular 401(k), Congress took steps to modify, but not eliminate, the plan. It agreed to allow the continued existence of the 401(k) but with limits: initially (in 1986) restricting employee annual contributions to $7,000, compared to $10,000 today. Benna—and millions of other American wage-earners—had won a huge victory that would forever change the face of investment savings.

Without Benna, I may not have ever become a 401(k) millionaire. Thanks, Ted.

The Demise of the Company Pension

Company pensions used to be pretty generous. In exchange for a lifetime of loyalty to a company like Chrysler or General Electric, an employee could count on a lavish pension that often paid 50 to 65 percent of preretirement salary. Toss in Social Security benefits and a modest savings plan, and many World War II generation Americans could retire in relative comfort.

In the early 1980s, technology had advanced to the point where companies found it easier to do business globally. Staffers in San Francisco could communicate easily with their counterparts in Singapore through the magic of networked computing. That was the good news. The bad news was that companies found they had to be more aggressive in marketing and distributing their goods and services in this competitive new global marketplace. That meant cutting costs—and the pricey company pension was a great place to start.

Employers began slashing their pension plans, leaving many employees fending for themselves in retirement. Enter the 401(k) plan, which came along at a convenient time for both management and workers. Through the 401(k) plan, employers could pass retirement responsibility to the employees themselves. For employers, all contributions made on behalf of employees were tax-deductible, including the salary-reduction contributions elected as 401(k) deferrals by employees. Savvy companies also began using the 401(k) benefit to recruit talented and loyal employees. Lower turnover translated into further cost reductions.

The Straight Skinny on Social Security

Employees also began to recognize that Social Security might not provide as much for their retirement as promised. The weight of the Social Security program is rapidly being shifted toward younger workers, fewer in number than previous generations who are already receiving their Social Security benefits. In 1950, there were as many as 16 workers for every Social Security retiree. Today there are only 3.2 workers for each beneficiary. According to the Social Security Board of Trustees, this ratio could fall as low as 2:1 by 2025.

To make matters worse, because people are living longer, you can expect to spend up to a quarter of your life (20 years or more) in retirement. With fewer workers paying in and more retirees taking out, the future health of Social Security hangs in the balance. Congress annually makes noises about raising the retirement age a year or two and boosting Social Security taxes to keep the Social Security system solvent.

Knute's Knotes

Percentage of Social Security That the Average Americans Will Get in Retirement

Financial experts estimate that Americans will need about 75 percent of their current annual income to maintain their preretirement lifestyle. And that doesn't account for inflation, which currently averages about 4 percent annually. Note that Social Security and pension benefits—if you're lucky enough to get pension benefits—will comprise only 43 percent of your retirement income. The other 57 percent will have to come from personal investments. That's where your 401(k) plan comes in.

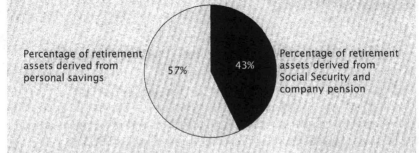

Percentage of retirement assets derived from personal savings — 57%

43% — Percentage of retirement assets derived from Social Security and company pension

Source: Social Security Administration and Bureau of Labor Statistics, 1997.

It has always been risky to depend on Social Security for your retirement needs. Since 1935, the Social Security system has been the foundation on which retirement plans are based. But it's only a bare-bones foundation. It was never intended to ensure a financially secure retirement all by itself. By taxing the current working population to pay the benefits of current retirees, Social Security simply provides a base on which you can build additional retirement security.

The Social Security Administration estimates that Social Security provides only about a quarter of what you can expect to pay for housing, food, and other living expenses—not to mention a birthday present or two for the grandkids. So it's really up to *you* to save and invest for your own future.

The Inflation Angle

Inflation never sleeps. What is inflation? It's the annual increase in the cost of goods and services, most often measured by the U.S. government's Consumer Price Index (CPI) that is released every month. Essentially, the CPI measures the "purchasing power"—and not the fixed value—of your money. In other words, as time passes and prices increase, your purchasing power is reduced.

Economic growth often causes moderate inflation by increasing consumer spending at a faster rate than the production of goods. In recent years, inflation has risen as high as 5 percent annually. That means a loaf of bread that cost $1.00 one year would cost $1.05 the next year. When too much money chases too few goods, inflation is the result.

As you contribute to your retirement savings, bear this in mind: you need to be sure that your retirement investments are staying ahead of inflation so that you'll have enough money to live comfortably in retirement—whenever that is. For example, if the inflation rate is 5 percent and you are saving $10,000 per year for your retirement, you need to increase your savings by 5 percent (or $500) for the next year (for a total of $10,500). The following year you'll have to save 5 percent of the $10,500, or $525, to keep up with the inflation.

Knute's Knotes

The Steady Rise of Inflation: A Comparison

Consider the rise in price of the following everyday goods from 1980 through 1995:

Item	1980	1995	Increase (Percent)
Postage stamp	15 cents	32 cents	113%
Levi's jeans	$11.02	$20.95	90
New car	$7,574	$19,600	159
Paperback book	$3.25	$5.95	83
The Wall Street Journal	30 cents	75 cents	150

Having $50,000 per year to live on in retirement may seem like plenty of money in 1998. But in 2028, that $50,000 will buy only half of what it's buying today.

The 401(k) Advantage

With fewer corporate pensions and a less secure Social Security, the 401(k) plan makes more and more sense as the cornerstone of your financial future. Let's take a closer look at the growth and advantages it offers.

The IRS doesn't hand out tax breaks easily. But since its introduction in 1980, the 401(k)—named after the section of the tax code that authorized it—has become America's most popular retirement benefit. There is no bigger tax break for the average American.

Through 1997, 25 million Americans have invested more than $1 trillion in 401(k) plans. Over 95 percent of companies with more than 5,000 employees offer these plans. By the year 2001, nearly 30 million workers at 340,000 companies nationwide will participate in a 401(k) plan that allows employees of corporations and private companies to save and invest for their own retirement. In 1996, Congress enabled noncorporate, tax-exempt organizations such as health care and educational institutions to join the list.

How does a 401(k) plan work? It's easy. Participating workers have a certain percentage of their paycheck—usually from 2 percent to 15 percent—deposited by their employer in a revenue-generating, tax-deferred investment account, which invests the cash in a range of stock, bond, and money-market mutual funds. All the investment income accumulates on a tax-deferred basis, and at age 59½ the employee is allowed to cash in on the 401(k) plan.

There is a legal limit to how much of your salary you can earmark for your 401(k). In 1998, the limit is $10,000, up $500 from 1997. This figure changes slightly from year to year and is usually pegged to an IRS indexed dollar amount, determined by a formula that's tougher to decipher than the one used to calculate your cable television bill. The Internal Revenue Service releases this dollar amount every year. Ask your human resources or employee benefits officer for the dollar figure every January and plan your 401(k) contributions to max out every year.

Knute's Knotes

The Folly of Taking Money Out of Your 401(k) Prior to Retirement

401(k)s are a great deal for everyone, but especially spendthrifts. The money you put away in a 401(k) is off-limits until you turn age 59½. The penalties are harsh for tapping into your account before you retire. First, you'll pay income tax on your investment and earnings. Second, as of 1996 you're penalized again by the IRS to the tune of 10 percent of the withdrawal. One other reason not to cash in early: if you borrow $10,000 to put in that hot tub you've been wanting and you then change jobs, you're in a bind. Your old company will want the money back in its entirety within 60 days of your leaving. And if you don't repay it both the IRS and your old company will nick you with fees and penalties that are so painful even the nicest hot tub won't cure them. To paraphrase Nike, my favorite brand of running shoe, "Just don't do it."

While Uncle Sam gives companies some flexibility in creating and customizing their 401(k) plans, they're fundamentally alike. Some plans differ in the amount of money an employer is willing to match or co-contribute. Other plans offer more investment options than others. But in general, they're the same.

According to the Department of Labor, there are over 142,000 company-sponsored 401(k) plans in operation today. The average plan offers participants six investment options and some sort of contribution matching (more on that later). You choose the percentage of your pretax pay that you can comfortably set aside (the more you contribute, the faster and higher your money grows). You control the account and a money manager hand-picked by your employer does the rest.

More in Your Pocket, Less in Uncle Sam's

The ample benefits of a 401(k) plan are immediate. Every dollar you contribute to your 401(k) means one less dollar that Uncle Sam can tax. The cash is deducted from your salary and placed into your 401(k) account before any federal, state, local, or Social Security taxes are taken out. Consequently, your payroll earnings reported to the IRS by your employer are decreased by the amount of your annual contribution. For example, if you earn $50,000 and invest $5,000 in pretax contributions to your 401(k) plan, your taxable salary is $45,000. If the IRS taxes your salary at a rate of 20 percent, your immediate federal and state income tax savings is $1,000 (see chart).

REDUCE YOUR TAXES TODAY

One-year tax savings for a $40,000 household income, with a federal tax bracket of 28 percent

	With 401(k)	Without 401(k)
Annual salary	$40,000	$40,000
401(k) contribution	−3,000	−0
Taxable earnings	$37,000	$40,000
Federal tax	−5,252	−6,092
Take-home salary	$31,748	$33,908
Amount saved in 401(k)	3,000	0
Total	$34,748	$33,908
Annual tax savings	$ 840	

Your employer may match some percentage of your contributions, providing you with an immediate return on your money. The average participating company matches 50 percent of the first 6 percent of the contribution you make into your 401(k) plan.

That's not all. Uncle Sam *gives* you *two* tax breaks in one package. In addition to the pretax allowance, the IRS also allows the money in your 401(k) plan to grow tax-free until you are ready to begin making withdrawals. The money your money makes via dividends, interest, and capital gains isn't taxed *as long as you reinvest the money into your 401(k) plan.*

And just watch that money grow! Through compound interest, your money grows all the time—while you're working, playing, eating, sleeping, or just daydreaming. And the more you put in your plan, the better you're going to live in retirement:

GROWTH RATE OF A 401(K) PLAN

The magic of compound interest: The longer you invest, the higher your money grows.

	Assume		
Annual Contribution of $2,000	5 Percent Return	8 Percent Return	13 Percent Return
10 Years	$ 25,156	$ 28,973	$ 36,839
20 Years	66,131	91,524	161,894
30 Years	132,878	226,566	586,398

The Perils of Procrastination

The earlier you start the better, giving your money more time to grow. Too many people say that they can't afford to save for retirement: There are mortgages to pay; children to feed, clothe, and educate; and other expenses.

But the idea that you can't live your life well, pay your bills, and save for retirement at the same time is bunk. Even though I never made those big six-figure salaries, and I had five kids to raise, I did it. While it's never too late to start saving for retirement, the sooner you begin an investment program, the longer time you have to achieve your goals with less immediate dollar expenses up front. In other words, the sooner you begin, the less it costs you to become a 401(k) millionaire.

A Word of Caution. The price you pay for procrastinating on your retirement savings is heavy indeed. Consider the story of two 25-year-olds, Melissa and Anthony. Melissa invests $2,000 a year over the first 10 years in her 401(k) and then stops, never adding a penny more to her portfolio for the next 30 years. She's a diligent investor who gets the standard 10 percent returns on her conservative mutual funds over the 40-year period, finally retiring with $607,695. Anthony, however, gets a late start but works hard to make up for lost time. Skipping the first nine years, he stashes $2,000 away in his 401(k) plan for the next 30 years. But even though Anthony takes three times as much money out of his own pocket as Melissa, his return is almost $250,000 less than hers, at $360,299. While both Anthony and Melissa have the power of compound interest on their side, Melissa harnessed it earlier and thus reaped higher gains.

The moral of the story? If you can afford to bypass tens or even hundreds of thousands of dollars in retirement money, by all means procrastinate.

Now consider a 25-year-old who saved $200 a month for 40 years (that's an investment of $96,000 over that timespan). By the time our 25-year-old turned 65, she'd have earned $1,542,254 on a return of 11 percent (the stock market average for the past 40 years). But if she'd started saving the same amount of money at age 55, and had only 10 years left until retirement, the numbers look grim: at the same investment return of 11 percent, she'd earn a paltry $44,210 on the $24,000 she managed to put away at that late age.

INVESTING $200 A MONTH
AT DIFFERENT STAGES OF LIFE
(Assuming 11 Percent Investment Return Annually)

	Amount Invested	Amount Earned by Age 65
Starting at age 55	$24,000	$ 44,210
Starting at age 45	48,000	170,078
Starting at age 35	72,000	527,469
Starting at age 25	96,000	1,542,254

401(k)s versus IRAs:
Who's This Roth Fella, Anyway?

The 401(k) is hardly your only tax-advantaged investment option. There's much to be said for Individual Retirement Accounts (IRAs), which promise many of the same benefits that you get from your 401(k).

A 401(k) is similar in many ways to an IRA, only stronger and more flexible. That doesn't mean IRAs aren't a good deal. No matter what your income, tax status, or how many retirement plans you participate in, you can always open an IRA. Through an IRA, you and your spouse can each contribute $2,000 of pretax income annually.

Starting in 1998, Americans can choose between two IRA options: the traditional IRA that provides tax-deferred growth and a potential tax deduction; and the Roth IRA, named after Delaware Senator William Roth, who sponsored the bill that enacted the new IRA. The primary difference between a regular IRA and a Roth IRA is that the money you contribute to a Roth IRA earns and compounds tax-free—you don't pay any current income tax on the interest, dividends, or capital gains earned. The contributions to a Roth IRA are not tax-deductible, and this type of IRA is available only if your joint adjusted gross income is below $160,000 ($110,000 if you're single). But the Roth IRA is accessible for tax-free withdrawals under certain conditions, such as to pay for some unreimbursed medical expenses or health insurance if you are unemployed or to pay for college tuition or a first home. There are limits and qualifications to each withdrawal scenario, but the benefit of the Roth IRA remains—your money is a little more available to you at critical points in life.

There's a big difference between *tax-free*, like the Roth IRA, and *tax-deferred*, like the IRA and 401(k). Like an IRA, you will pay taxes when you withdraw the money from your 401(k) at retirement, but again, you'll likely do so in a lower tax bracket than the one you're in now.

There are merits of the 401(k) over the IRAs. First, you can contribute more money annually—up to $10,000 for a 401(k) versus $2,000 for an IRA. Second, the tax-deferral versus tax-free gap really isn't as big as you might think. While you can deduct your $2,000 in some cases, you have to wait until the following April 15th to realize the benefits of your deduction. That money is put to better use in a 401(k), which gives you tax savings every pay period and puts your money to work for you in the financial markets all year long. If that $2,000 deduction from an IRA were instead put to use in a 401(k) growth stock mutual fund that returned 20 percent, you'd earn $400 you wouldn't have with an IRA.

Think of a 401(k) as an IRA's bigger brother. It offers more flexibility than IRAs and allows you to contribute a lot more money to your retirement every year. Plus, since Congress, in 1986, limited the deductions on IRAs to special cases (i.e., those who weren't covered by a retirement plan or couldn't afford an IRA), a lot of the teeth have been taken out of IRAs as a tax shelter.

Perhaps your best use of an IRA is when you've maxed out on your 401(k) and want to continue pouring tax-advantaged cash into your retirement. Once you've hit the $10,000 investment limit on your 401(k), putting an additional $2,000 into an IRA is a great idea.

403(b) Plans and Other Strangers

Public schools and nonprofit agencies cannot participate in 401(k)s, but do have something called a *403(b) plan*. It offers many of the same tax breaks as 401(k)s, but there are some differences. Employers, for example, are much less likely to offer matching funds in 403(b) plans. 403(b)s also emphasize annuities as their investment plan foundations, which have significantly higher expenses than the mutual funds used by 401(k) plans. If your 403(b) does offer mutual funds, and more and more do every day, it's a good idea to make the leap from annuities to funds. What you lose in surrender charges (the fees annuity providers charge to let you out of an annuity), you'll probably make up in better-performing mutual funds.

Federal, state, and local government employees are eligible for *457 plans*. Again, they provide the tax deferral of a 401(k) but not the employee match. Maximum limits are usually lower on 457s (up to $7,500) and the money you invest is classified by the government as *deferred compensation*. That's a fancy way of saying the money is Uncle Sam's, not yours—at least until you retire. So in the unlikely event of your city or municipality going bankrupt (it happened in Orange County, California) you're out of luck. That said, I think the slight risk of municipal bankruptcy is outweighed by the tax-deferral advantages. So sign up if you can.

Knute's Knotes

Top Five Reasons to Max Out on Your 401(k)

1. *401(k)s Force You to Save:* Putting money aside for future use is never easy. But a 401(k) makes it easier by forcing you to sock money away every pay period for your retirement. Most companies have automatic reduction plans that take money out of your gross, pre-tax earnings before you lay eyes on your paycheck. How can you miss something you never had?

2. *401(k)s Help You Save on Taxes:* While a 401(k) can't stop the taxman altogether, it does take a lot of wind out of his sails. Because your contributions are made with pre-tax dollars, you don't pay taxes on the money you invest in your 401(k). Imagine that! An IRS-sanctioned way that costs you less to save for your retirement.

3. *401(k)s Give You Flexibility:* Just because you reach age 59 1/2 and become eligible to cash in your 401(k), that doesn't mean you have to. In fact, you can gain further tax benefits on your retirement savings at that time by transferring your 401(k) stash to an IRA or other tax-advantaged retirement plan without losing your tax-deferred benefits, which ensures your money can keep growing tax-deferred throughout retirement. And these days, when many Americans live 25 or even 30 years in retirement, that money will come in handy.

4. *401(k)s Put the Miracle of Compounding in Your Corner:* I can't say enough about the advantages of compound interest. It enables your money to grow and grow over time. A 25-year-old legal secretary who places 10% of her $35,000 salary into her 401(k) every year until she

retires, and who earns a modest 10% return on her investments, will have more than $3 million waiting for her in retirement. Short of winning the lottery, show me a better deal.

5. *401(k)s Give You Free Money Through Employee Matching:* Most companies offer some sort of employee matching, and one out of four employers match contributions dollar for dollar up to specified levels. That's free, tax-deferred money for your retirement, courtesy of your employer.

A recurring theme throughout this book is the critical importance of investing early and often in your 401(k). Unless you get the benefits of time and compounded interest working for you, and the advantage of maxing out on your 401(k) contributions, chances are you won't become a 401(k) millionaire.

One of the best ways of ensuring that you'll get the most from your 401(k) plan is to understand how it works. That's what we'll cover in Chapter 3—everything from what to do when you receive your 401(k) packet to how to maximize your employee match benefit and how to minimize 401(k) management fees.

A 401(K) MAKEOVER

Name: Wilma N.

Age: 30

Occupation: Insurance company claims adjuster

Retirement Goals: First, I want to take care of my twin six-year-old boys' college funding. I don't know if it's wiser to save separately for college or to borrow money from my 401(k). After that, I hope to retire comfortably by age 60 or 65.

401(k) Assets: $15,000

Portfolio: 33% Aggressive growth fund
34% Growth and income fund
33% Long-term U.S. Treasury bond fund

Stocks: None

Comments: I just started investing in my 401(k) two years ago after my divorce. I wanted to be sure I had something put away in case I needed it. I'm really happy and surprised at how fast my money is growing even in the short time I've been a 401(K) investor. I hope to keep it up.

Knute Says

They say that knowing what your goals are is a big step in getting there. So that takes care of your first step. The next step is putting as much money as you can afford into all of your tax-deferred accounts—IRA, 401(k), and educational IRA. Your next step is to be more aggressive with your investments. College costs in 12 years will be about five times what they are now. Will you be able to afford it? With Pell Grants, student loans, state colleges, and so on, you may. Rather than borrow from your 401(k), try for all of the "free" money you're eligible for and then try to borrow the rest with a low-cost student loan. At this stage your portfolio should look like this:

40% Aggressive growth fund
20% International stick fund
20% Large cap growth fund
20% Small cap growth fund

3

The best way to get ahead is to get started.

—Mark Twain

The 401(k) Plan:
A Look Under the Hood

401(k)s are helping make Americans wealthier than ever. 401(k) millionaires, in fact, are sprouting up all over. If you don't believe me, ask the employees of T. Rowe Price, the big mutual fund company out of Baltimore, Maryland. At the end of 1995, company records showed a total of 120 millionaires out of 700,000 company-supported retirement plans managed by the company. Eighteen months later, the number of millionaires rose by 250 percent to 308, while the number of plan accounts only grew to 870,000. To put those numbers in context, how many average Americans have retired lately as millionaires thanks to their company pensions or to Social Security? None, I'd wager.

Imagine that! Over 300 401(k) millionaires in one fund company alone! Only 20 years ago, 75 percent of employee benefit plans promised "fixed benefits" (that's why the old pension plans are still referred to as "defined benefits" plans), no matter how the stock market performed. 401(k) plans, in which employees invest their money with the help of plan providers, changed all that. Often referred to by human resources directors and Washington bureaucrats as "defined contribution" plans, because the contributions, and not the benefits, are fixed, 401(k) plans have more than tripled in value from 1986 to

1997—to $1.5 trillion, according to the Employee Benefit Research Institute in Washington, D.C.

As a result, employers, only too happy to promote a plan that makes employees wealthy and takes firms off the hook for providing company-funded pensions, are adding more choices and options to 401(k) plans. Until only a few years ago the average 401(k) plan was limited to three or four investment choices: a stock mutual fund, a bond mutual fund, a money market mutual fund, and some company stock. Responding to consumer demand for more investment options, employers are now offering up to two or three dozen 401(k) investment options, like stock index, international, and emerging market funds. Eastman Kodak recently began offering a whopping thirty-six 401(k) plan options, including country- and region-specific funds and industry-specific funds in the high technology and pharmaceutical sectors. There, company officials said that the proposal was no different than what the rest of corporate America was doing: shifting more toward broader investment options and placing an even greater emphasis on employee responsibility. Part and parcel of the increased 401(k) packages is also a greater emphasis on stock investing, where the rewards—and the risks—are greater than with more conservative investments like bonds.

While the move by corporate America to expand plan options is big, the trend toward greater investment options is more reflective of workers' recognition that the 401(k) plan can potentially make them rich. But moving from "recognizing" the potential to "understanding" how 401(k)s work is a giant leap that many 401(k) investors haven't taken yet. Unfortunately, many Americans currently participating in 401(k)s don't understand them. In fact, according to a 1997 Merrill Lynch survey of 401(k) plan participants, only 50 percent said they felt comfortable in their knowledge of the plans.

Getting to Know You

Squeezing the most performance out of your 401(k) is easy if you know how. And knowing how means knowing what your 401(k) plan is all about. So let's see what makes it tick.

The Paperwork

When you sign up to participate in your company's 401(k) plan, expect some paperwork. Fortunately, it's not as onerous as what you might expect from the IRS or your local Registry of Motor Vehicles, but it can be substantial. Don't skip over your plan package, the bulky folder you get from your human resources department detailing your 401(k) plan. Inside is the stuff you need to know to maximize your participation—and remuneration—in the plan.

Your paperwork will detail the general rules, terms, and investment options that apply to your plan. Key items to look for are how much, if any, your company will match; your investment options; your fee structure (your company and plan manager probably don't want you to know it, but you do get charged for the administration of your plan); and your loan and withdrawal options. Each quarter you'll receive your plan statement, often accompanied by a newsletter from your plan provider. Unlike *The Wall Street Journal* or subscriber-oriented investment newsletters, these fund letters are glorified sales pitches. Some can cost up to $300,000 per year to produce. That money doesn't come out of the fund companies' pocket, it comes out of yours in the form of higher 401(k) management fees. Keep the statement and file it along with your other financial documents, preferably in a safe, bank deposit box, or other, similarly secure and dry place. Drop the newsletter in the trash.

Knute's Knotes

The Top Five 401(k) Recordkeepers

Even though your employer may keep an employee benefits staff on hand to assist you with questions about your 401(k), your plan records aren't kept with your company. Instead, they're kept with the financial services company that serves as your company's 401(k) plan provider. All charge fees (we'll get to that in a minute), and some are better than others. But according to professional investors, if you see any of the following companies listed as your plan provider, your plan is being handled by the best. The first list encompasses overall 401(k) plan administration, that is, performance, fees, fund options. The second list is based strictly on performance:

1. Fidelity Investments
2. The Vanguard Group
3. Cigna
4. Hewitt Associates
5. The Principal Financial Group

Sooner or later, it's all about money. Since 401(k) participants can't manage the funds they choose for their portfolios, it helps to have fund managers on hand who do a great job making money for investors. These companies have proven to be the top performing 401(k) investment management companies in the United States (i.e., they're making more money for plan participants than anyone else). If your money is being managed by these guys, chances are it's in good hands:

1. Fidelity Investments
2. The Vanguard Group
3. Cigna
4. T. Rowe Price
5. Merrill Lynch

Source: Judy Diamond Associates.

Plan Dates

Normally, your 401(k) plan has its own accounting timetable. Most plans operate from the traditional January 1 through December 31 cycle but some (for company bookkeeping reasons) may be operating on a different calendar, say from April 1 to March 31 of the following year. These plan dates come into play if you need to borrow funds (which I hope you don't) or otherwise withdraw the money (which I know you won't until after you reach age 59½). Your withdrawal options are based on your years of service to the firm; and some firms don't start counting those years of service on your employment date, but the accounting dates that the plan adheres to. For example, if you wanted to borrow money from your 401(k), your company may have a provision that you can borrow funds only after one full year with the firm. And it's the plan date—not your first day on the job—that dictates what a "full" year is.

The Deduction Dates: When Is My Money Taken Out?

You can count on your 401(k) contribution being deducted every time you get paid—whether that's once a month, biweekly, or weekly. And unless you're not working with a good, sound budget and are struggling with your cash flow, you'll barely notice the difference in your paycheck.

The best part is that the deduction from your paycheck is from your *gross* income and not your *net* income. Remember when I told you in Chapter 2 that your 401(k) plan money is taken out pretax—or before Uncle Sam gets his share? What that means is simple: If your biweekly paycheck amounts to $800 and you contribute $100 of it to your 401(k) plan, your take home pay will only decrease by about $80 even though you put $100 into your plan.

When Do I Qualify to Participate?

Every company has its own rules, but usually you can begin participating in a 401(k) plan within 30 days of being hired. Some companies may insist you stick around for six months to a year before you're eligible. If you're new on the job, or even interviewing for a new post, ask the human resources director or your employee benefits specialist when 401(k) eligibility kicks in.

A word on enrollment. Don't be discouraged if you fill out your 401(k) plan paperwork and then find out you have to wait 30 days to officially begin participating in your plan. For bookkeeping and money management reasons, both on the part of your employer and your plan provider, 30 days is what it takes to get your plan rolling. You can make up the lost month with a heftier annual contribution!

How Much Can I Give?

The Federal government has treated 401(k) plan contributions like a yo-yo in the past. Prior to 1986, employees could contribute up to $30,000. In 1987, that amount was reduced to $7,000 (ouch!) to conform with onerous new tax laws that eliminated a lot of tax shelters. Currently, the government has tied increases in the 401(k) cap to inflation and the Consumer Price Index, Uncle Sam's barometer of inflation. Since 1987, the contribution limits have risen from $7,000 to $10,000.

The rules also give some discretion to companies to allow employees to contribute a certain percentage of their income, as long as it doesn't exceed the $10,000 (as of 1998) limit. Most companies limit those contributions to 15 percent of an employee's total taxable income. But under the current $10,000 limit, an employee would have to earn about $65,000 to reach the $10,000 contribution level. That's not easy in a country where the average worker earns $30,000 annually. Some companies, recognizing the unfairness of the contribution limits, allow employees to contribute 20 percent of their total income to their 401(k) plan.

"But what about my company pension?" you ask? The government has stipulations on all employer-sponsored retirement plans. If your company offers you several retirement plan options, you can't contribute more than 25 percent of your taxable income, or $30,000, whatever is less. For you minimalists out there—and I hope you change your stripes after reading this book—you can usually contribute a minimum of 1 percent or 2 percent to your 401(k) plan. Anything less and your employer probably won't allow it. Funding and administering 401(k) plans isn't a profit generator for your bosses, and they don't want to administer a 401(k) plan for people who contribute pennies a year.

Knute's Knotes

Top-Tier Companies When It Comes to Contributing to Employees' 401(k) Plans

Consider yourself lucky to work at a company that offers generous 401(k) benefits. The participating employees at the following companies are whistling a happy tune:

Best Company Match
(Maximum Percent of Employee's Salary Matched)

Ford Motor	10%
McDonald's	10%
Textron	10%

Some companies recognize that it's hard to save money when employees aren't making a whole lot of it. That's why it's refreshing to see firms aggressively matching lower income earning employees' contributions. The thinking? The companies are trying to incentivize employees at lower wage levels who find it difficult to contribute even the smallest percentage of their salary:

Companies That Reward Lower Income Earners
by Matching More Than $1 for $1

Dayton Hudson	$1 for $1 Match up to 5% of Pay
The Gap	$1 for $1 Match up to 4% of Pay
Walgreen's	$2.64 per $1 Match up to 2% of Pay

Source: *USA Today.*

What's the Company Match?

Company matches are like sunny days in May: welcome and plentiful. But your company's not matching your 401(k) contributions because they're nice guys. A big reason that employee matches are made at all is to comply with federal regulations on participation levels in 401(k)s. That means that if the lower paid workers aren't participating in a company 401(k) plan, then the higher-paid executives can't contribute as much as they like. The Labor Department runs constant tests and formulas to make sure that *all* company employees, from clerks to CEOs, are participating in the 401(k) plan on roughly equal percentage levels. (Despite the government's best efforts, the gap between executives and blue-collar workers is growing wider. According to KPMG Peat Marwick, a top-notch accounting firm, 90 percent of highly paid workers contribute to their 401(k) plans compared with 64 percent of all other workers.)

The employee match is good news for employers and employees alike. Consider Digital Equipment Corporation: The computer giant found that after adding a matching contribution to its 401(k) in 1995, plan participation shot up 72 percent. So now both boardroom barons and back-office buckaroos are better off.

While some company matches may come in the form of company stock or other noncash items, most matches are in cash. In fact, according to the Washington, D.C. research firm of Hewitt & Associates, over 80 percent of American companies offer some form of company cash matching to employees participating in their 401(k) plans. Some companies are generous, forking over 100 percent of your plan contributions. Seattle-based Pemco Financial Services gets my employer-of-the-year award for awarding employees 200 percent matching up to the first 6 percent of compensation contributed to an employee's 401(k) plan. Wow.

Other companies are more Scrooge-like, parceling out only 10 percent or 15 percent of employee contributions. Most, as I said, contribute on average about 50 percent of employee's 401(k) plan contributions yearly, usually up to certain contribution limits. Still, 50 percent of every dollar you contribute means an automatic 50 percent return on your 401(k) investment. Most top-performing mutual funds don't average 20 percent returns annually, so if you're like me, you go to bed each night giving thanks to the 401(k)'s employee match provision.

The company match is a big reason why you should always max out your 401(k); if you don't contribute the 6 percent limit that the average employer co-funds, you're missing out on free money. If you contribute, say, only 3 percent of your annual salary to your 401(k) plan, and your employer is willing to match your contribution up to 6 percent, you're missing out on 50 percent of what your employer is willing to give you. Free! Gratis! No charge! On the house!

Put it this way. What would your bosses' response be if you walked into her office and announced, "I've got a great idea! Why don't you give me 3 percent of my annual salary for free?" How soon before she calls the men in white jackets? But placed in the context of your 401(k) plan, she's only too glad to fork over the cash. Think about that when you're considering the contribution amounts you want to make to your 401(k) plan every year.

A few caveats on company matching. Some matching plans come with strings attached. An employer, for example, may tie the company match contribution to an agreement on your part to invest in the firm's far riskier company stock instead of a safer mutual fund. It's usually not a good idea to invest in too much company stock. We'll cover that in greater detail in Chapter 5 when we discuss 401(k) plan investment options.

Or your employer may make the matching contribution contingent on your staying with the company for a fixed number of years. In employee benefit circles, that's known as "vesting," where you have to stay a predetermined number of years with the company before you can lay final claim to the money that the company has been contributing to your 401(k) all along. Your own personal contributions to your 401(k) are always yours and yours alone.

Fees and Expenses: A Big Heads-Up

There are charges that 401(k) plan participants incur. Don't expect the Fidelity Investments or the Vanguard Funds of the world to manage billions of dollars in 401(k) plans out of the goodness of their hearts. Most 401(k) plan participants don't even know that they're paying fees. And studies show that 401(k) plan administration fees are rising. According to HR Investment Consultants, at companies with 100 employees, annual 401(k) plan fees have risen to $54 in 1998 from $49 in 1995. Some companies are making even more gravy from *investment fees*—the cost of managing your 401(k) plan's investments by financial services companies—by charging well over 1 percent of your total plan assets in commissions for themselves. According to *Money Magazine*, one investment company, Zurich Kemper Life, was snatching 2.2 percent of 401(k) plan participants' total plan assets annually in investment management fees. That means if your 401(k) portfolio was worth $100,000, the management fee taken out of your plan assets would be $2,200. That's too much!

Your 401(k) administrative booklet that was provided to you when you joined the plan should include the total amount of fees you're paying for your participation in the plan. If you don't see it there, check with your plan administrator or your human resources representative.

Some of these fees come in the form of what Wall Street calls "12B-1" fees—monies charged consumers for the costs that financial services companies incur in marketing their mutual funds to you, such as advertising and marketing costs. (Remember the fund company newsletter I told you about? You're paying for it through increased 12B-1 fees.)

Your employer may even be benefiting from the 12B-1 fees that you're paying the plan provider. According to *The Wall Street Journal*, many employers have an incentive to choose the more expensive funds with 12B-1 fees, because they get breaks from the plan provider in the form of free or reduced record-keeping charges. In other words, your boss is taking the money you paid your 401(k) plan provider and sticking it back into his own pocket without (he hopes) you knowing. Worse, they're choosing the more expensive funds with the 12B-1 fees attached just to get the free record-keeping that comes with them.

One way to find out if your company has such a deal with a fund company is to ask your employee benefits director what fee arrangements exist between your company and 401(k) plan providers. I know of one worker in Seattle who approached her boss and pointed out that their 401(k) costs were twice as high as a competitive financial services firm with better investment performance. The boss, realizing that his own 401(k) was suffering as a result, made the switch to the better-performing fund company.

My rule is if you're paying more than 1 percent of your plan assets in 401(k) management fees, you're getting a raw deal.

Knute's Knotes

According to HR Investment Consultants, a Baltimore-based employee benefits consultancy, fees for 401(k) plan management are as varied as the items at an all-you-can-eat buffet. In a study of plans that cover an average of 500 employees, investment companies charge up to nearly 3 percent for 401(k) management fees:

Lowest cost providers: 0.53% ($159 annually on the average $30,000 balance)
Highest cost provider: 2.56% ($768 annually on the average $30,000 balance)

Source: HR Investment Consultants and Dow Jones Newswire.

Loanheads Are Boneheads: The Folly of Taking Your Money Out of Your 401(k)

Even though I think you should walk over a bed of red-hot coals before you borrow from your 401(k), I'd be remiss in not telling you how to do it. You never know when a real emergency will arise, and the money to pay for it has to come from somewhere.

Most 401(k) plans do allow you to take a loan from your plan. According to the Profit Sharing/401(k) Council of America, 84 percent of all 401(k) plan members can borrow from their 401(k)s. About 30 percent do so, borrowing on average 10 percent of their plan holdings. It's perfectly legal, although, in most cases, there are moderate tax penalties involved. In fact, the only good thing about a 401(k) loan is that it beats taking an early withdrawal from your 401(k) plan. The tax considerations that stirs up are truly onerous.

Usually you can borrow up to $50,000, or half of your plan's account balance, and you'll probably pay one or two percentage points above normal bank lending rates for the privilege of borrowing your own money. You'll also likely pay a small processing fee of anywhere from 1 percent to 5 percent of the loan to the plan provider, who'll be handling your paperwork. As I just mentioned, almost anyone who participates in a 401(k) plan can borrow from it and, since there's no bank involved and it's your money, you ultimately wind up paying yourself back for the loan. The legal time limit for 401(k) loan paybacks is five years, although the government says that if you borrow the funds to buy your primary residence you can have a "reasonable" amount of time to pay the money back.

One exception: If you leave your job and owe money on a loan from your 401(k), your company can—and probably will—come after you hard for the money. Even though it's technically your money, your ex-employer will want to close the books on your tenure with the company. The IRS insists that 401(k) loans be paid back within 60 days of leaving a company. Anything after that is treated as an early withdrawal and taxed accordingly.

While at first glance the 401(k) loan doesn't sound like such a bad deal, take a closer look. When you borrow money from your 401(k) plan, you're taking money that was working for you in the stock market and putting it to use in the consumer market. The idea of 401(k) investing is that it makes you a saver, *not a consumer*. Sure, you can take money out to buy a new car, but the money you take out doesn't just symbolize the price of the car. It symbolizes that price plus the amount of money you're going to lose on missed-out compound interest. It just doesn't make any sense.

Remember what I said earlier about taking a $10,000 loan and then leaving your job (or, worse, getting laid off)? If you can't pay it back, the IRS considers that money a "premature distribution" from your 401(k) and taxes you on the money plus a 10 percent interest penalty.

Even if you do pay the money back, the tax bite can still hurt in some cases. When you take a loan from your 401(k), you pay taxes twice on the money you borrow. The cash you use to pay back the loan is made with after-tax dollars. That means money you have already paid taxes on (when you earned it through your job) will be taxed again when you take it back out of your plan after retirement.

Remember, your 401(k) is a retirement account, *not* a savings account. Even though the government has loosened restrictions on 401(k) borrowing that make the plans look more and more like savings accounts every day, I'm here to tell you that any good derived from taking a loan from your 401(k) is emphatically canceled out when you consider the earning-power damage you'd be inflicting by removing that money. Just look at the amazing performance of the stock market during the past three years. If you took a loan out of your 401(k) in 1995, you would have lost the critical accumulation that 90 percent stock market returns over the past three years would have given you. And that's money you'll never make back, ever.

Knute's Knotes

Saving for your kids' college fund? Thinking about tapping your 401(k) account for the money? Think again. Even though Uncle Sam does allow for early 401(k) withdrawals for a college bill due in the next 12 months under the "safe harbor" laws, it's not a good idea.

Remember, your 401(k) money is for your retirement. Uncle Sam wants it that way and will tax you silly if you try to take it out early. So instead of your 401(k), try contacting these helpful organizations, all of whom want to see your children go on to college and are willing to help you make it happen:

College Board (Phone: 212-713-8000; www.collegeboard.org)
College Scholarship Service (Phone: 609-771-7725; www .collegeboard.org)
FAFSA Questions and Information (Phone: 319-337-5665)
Federal Student Aid Hotline (U.S. Department of Education) (Phone: 800-433-3243)
Student Loan Aid Hotline (SALLIE MAE) (Phone: 800-831-LOAN)

Roll Over, Beethoven: What to Do When You Leave Your Job

One day you're toiling away at your desk, minding your own business, when an old friend calls out of the blue to offer you a new job with easier hours, a juicier job description, and a 25 percent pay increase. Two weeks later, after 10 years with the same company, you find yourself taking a different route to a different job with a different outlook on life. That's the good news.

But let me be the first to tell you that switching jobs can have a lasting, not always favorable, impact on your 401(k) plan if you're not careful. Uncle Sam gives you 60 days to make up your mind about what you want to do with your 401(k) plan money. The choices are these: You can keep the money in your old 401(k) plan, which is sort of pointless because you're no longer able to contribute to the plan. Or you can move your contributions to the next company's 401(k) plan or switch to a special IRA. If you, in a monumental fit of stupidity, elect not to roll the money over into your new employer's 401(k) or another IRA account and keep the money yourself, your old employer will cut you a check for the proceeds minus 20 percent for taxes. Paying the IRS 20 percent of anything is bad enough. But giving up the tax-deferred, interest-compounding benefits of one-fifth of your 401(k) assets is worse than shortsighted!

Unfortunately, plenty of otherwise rational Americans take the money from their 401(k)s when they leave a job and spend it. In a 1995 study released by the U.S. Department of Labor, 68 percent of the Americans over the age of 40 who changed jobs cashed out on their 401(k). And a staggering 84 percent under the age of 40 took the money instead of rolling it over into another tax-deferred investment plan. This is sheer lunacy.

Consider the case of Buddy, a 35-year-old salesman who changed jobs. So far, Buddy had only accumulated $5,000 in his former company's 401(k)—not much by his standards. So Buddy figured he wouldn't miss the money and took it out to splurge on a new set of golf clubs and a big-screen TV.

But what if Buddy had rolled the money over into his new company's 401(k) plan? If he had, and the money had earned a moderate 8 percent annually with all dividends and capital gains reinvested, he could have had $33,000 when he retired at age 59½. Poor Buddy. That was an expensive TV set.

When (and How) Do I Get My Money After Retirement?

In most cases, the IRS does not allow you to take withdrawals from your 401(k) until you reach age 59½ without punishing you taxwise. For those age 55 or over who are disabled, laid off, or quit their jobs, special dispensations are allowed, but you are responsible for federal income taxes on any 401(k) withdrawals, unless you roll over your 401(k) plan money into an IRA.

When you retire and take your 401(k) plan distribution, you have the option of taking all the money in a lump sum or in increments, usually in the form of a monthly annuity. An annuity is an investment contract sold by a life insurance company that offers tax-deferral on investment growth and income and that offers you a guaranteed lifetime payment stream. Annuities can be fixed, meaning that your monthly income remains the same through the lifetime of the investment contract; or variable, meaning that your annuity is tied to an investment index, like the Standard & Poor's 500 Index, and changes from month to month. (Be careful about fixed annuities. As their value remains static every year, inflation will erode it over time.)

Taking the money in a lump sum provides you with a decent tax break in most cases. Through a tax provision called "five-year averaging," the government essentially provides you with a lower tax bill for paying the tax on your lump-sum investment up front instead of incrementally through annual IRA distributions throughout your retirement.

If you die, your spouse or heirs will receive all the 401(k) distributions that were due to you. If you haven't designated a beneficiary for your 401(k) in the event of your death, do so immediately. If you are married, your spouse, by default, will inherit the money. If you're not married, you may designate the beneficiary or beneficiaries of your choice. If you don't, your friends and relatives may fight over the money and the courts may have to intervene. You don't want that to happen.

A "no" answer to any of these questions may mean you're not getting all you can from your 401(k).

Knute's Knotes

Believe it or not, the IRS is in your corner when it comes to taking money out of your 401(k) plan after retirement with minimal tax bite. The IRS offers several publications geared toward making the withdrawal process easier and less expensive than ever. Others do as well:

- Individual Retirement Arrangements; Publication 575, Pension and Annuity Income, and Publication 560, Retirement Plans for the Self-Employed. Call (800) TAX-FORM for copies.
- Salomon Smith Barney, the New York City-based financial giant, offers two similar publications: The

Direct Rollover IRA and IRA Distribution Manual. Call (800) 424-3209, ext. 5484 for copies.
- The American Association of Retirement People (AARP) offers "A Guide to Understanding Your Pension Plan" and "How to Plan Your Successful Retirement." Contact AARP at their Washington, D.C., headquarters for copies: (202) 434-2277; www.aarp.org.

Knute's Knotes

How Does Your 401(k) Plan Measure Up? Check the Following List to See:

1. Does your plan provide you with the opportunity to sign up immediately after you're hired?
2. Does your employer provide at least a 50 percent employee match to some or all of your contributions?
3. Does your 401(k) plan provide at least six investment options?
4. Can you get timely account information via computer or 24-hour 1-800 telephone?
5. Do you have the flexibility to make transfers or change allocations at least four times annually?
6. Are the total expenses of your 401(k) plan no more than 1 percent of your plan assets?

A 401(K) MAKEOVER

Name: Joan D.

Age: 56

Occupation: Office manager at plumbing company

Retirement Goal: Retire at age 62. Save enough money to buy vacation home in Florida and contribute to grandchildren's education.

401(k) Assets (Through June, 1998): $456,300

Portfolio: 35% Stable value fund
15% Conservative equity income
15% Equity index fund
15% Growth stock fund
10% International stock fund
10% Aggressive growth fund

Stocks: Johnson & Johnson; General Electric; Hewlett Packard

Comments: I started early, although I wasn't maxing out on my 401(k) until my mid-40s. But the aggressive approach I adopted in my 401(k) has really paid off. I wonder, though, if I should start pulling back and becoming more conservative since I'm getting closer to retirement.

Knute Says

You've done a great job aggressively diversifying your 401(k) portfolio but now with 6 years to go until retirement you should begin to make your holdings more conservative. Over the next year or two, I would start putting some more into intermediate term bond funds. By the time you retire in 6 years, you should have about ½ your money in a bond fund. I would eliminate the agressive growth fund and allocate your portfolio as follows:

50 percent Intermediate bond fund
5 percent International stock fund
10 percent S&P 500 index fund
20 percent Stable value fund
10 percent Conservative equity income fund
5 percent Growth stock fund

Keep maxing out on your 401(k) contributions and when you retire enjoy your grandchildren in your Florida vacation home. I know I do.

4

*If you don't know where you're
going, any road will take you there.*

—A Wise Man

Investor, Know Thyself

When my wife and I got married in the 1960s, we didn't have a
problem combining our furniture. Our problem was that we had
to combine our debts. We were both living beyond our incomes and
had lots of credit card debt. After the honeymoon, the first thing we did
was set up (and stick to) a budget. This was the smartest financial move
I'd ever made. Figuring out where our money was going helped crys-
tallize our attitude about money—a critical first step in making plans
for the future.

So now that you've learned a little something about your 401(k),
let's consider *your* attitude about money and how that attitude will
translate into a lifetime financial plan built around your 401(k). Taking
stock of your personal financial situation is a vital step in becoming a
401(k) millionaire. It's a blueprint you'll be using the rest of your working years. Determining what you need to live on in retirement, mar-
shaling your resources, establishing a budget, and setting an ultimate
goal for your golden years may seem like daunting tasks at first. But
they don't have to be if you're prepared.

Setting a Budget

Most Americans will spend about 90,000 hours working in a lifetime.
Who wouldn't look forward to retiring? Yet few spend so much as an

hour a month planning for this time and tracking the progress of the plan. So it's not surprising that when things go awry, when financial goals aren't met, and their retirement plan isn't growing as fast as they would like, people get upset.

Many times the source of an insufficient retirement plan is an insufficient budget. It's hard to make a regular habit of putting money away into your 401(k) plan if you're buried under a mountain of monthly bills. Most of us have to pay a mortgage, some insurance, a car payment or two, and other needs. But why do so many of us insist on living in an expensive house when a modest one will do, or driving a Range Rover when a Buick will suffice? Why are we so materialistic?

Materialism is one of the major obstacles to meeting your retirement goals. Expensive cars and big mortgages are budget busters, as are dining out frequently and closets full of designer clothes. If you don't live within your means, then you can't and won't reach your lifetime financial goals. Remember, every $1 you put into your 401(k) plan when you are 25 can be $250 when you retire. Do the math!

Let's map out a budget plan that makes sense for you, leaves you room for fun and frolic, and gives you a realistic shot at retiring comfortably. Here's how it works.

Take Control

Ted Turner or Donald Trump may need a financial advisor but you and I don't. Managing your own budget is better than hiring a financial planner to do it for you. First, you save money on the fee you'd pay the advisor. Second, you'll gain the confidence, knowledge, and skill needed to manage your financial affairs in life.

Start by gathering all your monthly bills and credit card and bank receipts for the past 12 months and log them into a notebook. Or, if you have a computer at home, use it. Financial software like Quicken's Financial Planner or Microsoft Money 98 can help and they're cheap—about $50 or less. Include the obvious, like mortgage, car, and insurance payments. Then add everything else you can think of: utility and phone bills, cable television, America Online or other Internet fees, food, entertainment, dry cleaning, and, if you've got kids in college, tuition bills. Then record every dime you spend for two months. After 60 days, you'll have a pretty good idea where your money is going.

Also keep tabs on your daily expenses. A cup of coffee and a Danish every day may cost only $2.50. But that adds up to $12.50 per week, $50 per month, or $600 per year. That's a lot of money! What about lottery tickets? I know people who buy $5 worth a day and never think twice about it (and never win). That money could be invested in a growth mutual fund or an education account for a son or daughter. Little expenses add up and while they may not be budget busters, they sure aren't working *for* you either.

Knute's All-Time Top Money-Saving Tips

1. If you're in the market for a new home, don't make the mistake of confusing the mortgage you qualify for with the amount you should spend. There's no rule that says you have to buy a home that conforms to your mortgage qualifications. In fact, hunt harder for your new home and spend $10,000 less. You'll probably wind up in the house you wanted all along. And you'll have more money to put away for your retirement.
2. If you get a salary increase, nobody is forcing you to spend it. Sure, celebrate over a nice dinner out or buy something special for the family. Then sock the increase in your pay away in your retirement plan and watch your money grow even faster.
3. Keep all your ATM withdrawal receipts from the bank. Without them, you'll find it difficult to track your expenses. With them, you've got an eye-opening paper

trail of exactly how much cash you're plowing through each month.

4. Get your spouse and family involved in budgeting and planning for important purchases. Everyone in your family has a stake. By involving your kids, you can teach them valuable lessons in financial responsibility.

5. Speaking of your kids, be sure to make room for fun in your budget. I'm a bulldog when it comes to saving a buck, but I like to have a good time, too. I always made room in our budget for a weekly dinner out with my family at a decent restaurant. I also made sure my kids had pocket money for CDs or whatever—I just did it sensibly. You're never going to meet your financial goals with an unrealistic budget, but you're never going to create a realistic budget unless you make room for some family fun. A wise man once told me that it is foolish to live poor and die rich.

6. Change is inevitable, except (in my experience) from a vending machine. Your car's engine dies, your daughter needs braces, your furnace breaks. Stuff happens! That's why it's important to set up an emergency fund equal to your living expenses for six months. That's right, six months. I realize six months' worth of pay is a good chunk of change and not easy to save. But just keep your expenses (especially your credit card bill) down and you'll get there soon enough. You'll be glad you did. Planning for the worst is simply good planning, and no family budget should be without an emergency fund. Keep the money in a money market account so you can earn some interest on it.

7. Don't get discouraged if you manage to put away only one-third or one-half of the money you intended to when you began your budget. Shortfalls happen to virtually everyone—including me—in the first year of a

new budget. As long as you stick to your budget plan, the money will begin accumulating soon enough. I remember putting 10 percent of my pay away when I first began a budget. After a while, I started to put more—almost as a dare to myself, to see how little we could live on comfortably. Soon I was socking away 20 percent of my pay, and we barely missed the extra money. When that happens, you're bound to get excited as you see how much more you can save. It's like a monthly game that you win every time.

Look at it this way. Even $10 a month is better than nothing. At an 8 percent annual rate of return, that amounts to $35,142 in 40 years. Not exactly chump change. So do it!

The following worksheet will help you tabulate where your money is going and give you an idea of the strides you can make in saving for retirement. Fill it out completely. When you're done, you'll have a firm grasp on your personal financial situation. These numbers don't lie.

Cash Flow Worksheet

INCOME			
Salary	_____	Pensions	_____
Spouse's salary	_____	Social Security	_____
Commissions	_____	Other retirement income	_____
Spouse's commissions	_____	Tax refunds	_____
Bonus	_____	Other	_____
Spouse's bonus	_____	Total Income	_____
Income from business	_____		
Dividends	_____	EXPENSES	
Interest	_____	*Home*	
Rent paid to you	_____	Mortgage or rent	_____
Income from trusts	_____	Electricity	_____
Gifts to you	_____	Gas	_____
Alimony received	_____	Water and sewer	_____

Cash Flow Worksheet (continued)

Telephone

Property taxes _____

Homeowner's
  insurance _____

Household help _____

Furniture _____

Other household items _____

Home maintenance _____

Other household
  maintenance costs _____

Other _____

Family

Food and grocery _____

Clothing _____

Laundry and dry
  cleaning _____

Toiletries _____

Medicine _____

Health care costs not
  covered by insurance _____

Child care _____

Children's camp _____

Birthday, holiday, and
  other gifts _____

Education _____

Health insurance _____

Dental expense _____

Dental insurance _____

Life insurance _____

Disability insurance _____

Other insurance
  expense _____

Other _____

TRANSPORTATION

Gasoline _____

Auto insurance _____

Auto registration _____

Auto maintenance _____

Auto registration _____

Other travel expense _____

Other _____

LEISURE

Vacations _____

Club memberships _____

Books and magazines _____

Movies and theater _____

Cable television _____

Restaurants _____

Other _____

INCOME TAXES

Federal withheld tax _____

Federal estimated _____

State withheld tax _____

State estimated _____

Other _____

Other Miscellaneous _____

Installment loans _____

Payroll savings _____

IRA contributions _____

Keogh contributions _____

401(k) contributions _____

Investment expenses _____

Attorney's fees _____

Accountant's fees _____

Charitable contributions _____

Political contributions _____

Other _____

Other _____

Other _____

Other _____

Total Expenses _____

Total Income _____

Less Total Expenses _____

Total Surplus (Shortfall) _____

Knute's Knotes

Pay Yourself First

Here's a riddle for you: Why do banks, phone companies, and mutual fund firms offer to draw the money you owe them directly from your checking account? Because they want to get paid right off the top, that's why.

Your budget should be treated no differently, so when you sit down to handle your monthly bills, pay yourself first. Take the amount of money you're setting aside each month—be it $10, $50, $100, $200, or $300—and stick it into a mutual fund account or into the stock market.

That's how your 401(k) money is deducted—straight from your paycheck. Even if you've maxed out on your 401(k) plan, don't spend the additional money you've saved. Open an IRA account with a mutual fund company and put that extra money to work right away.

Think of yourself as your biggest creditor and pay yourself first. It's the most satisfying bill you'll pay all month.

Get Out of Debt

Once you've established where your money is going, start making plans to eliminate your debt. I read a *Wall Street Journal* article recently about a fellow who had amassed $40,000 in credit card debt. He recognized the folly of paying 20 percent interest a month to his card provider and set out to wipe out the debt. Good for him. But to do so, he borrowed money from his 401(k), figuring that it was better to pay himself the interest rather than pay someone else. Wrong.

I can't argue with the need for doing whatever it takes to reduce your credit card debt, but it was a mistake to put his retirement fund in jeopardy to do so. Let's examine $40,000 in credit card debt, spread out among four cards. At a 18 percent interest rate, his annual interest bill would come to about $7,200 ($40,000 multiplied by 0.18). Insane.

The moral of the story? If you have credit card debt, pay it off. Even taking a loan at the current rate of around 8 percent and paying the debt is much better than borrowing against your 401(k) and decreasing its earning power or continuing to pay the higher interest rates that credit card companies charge. Better yet, never overuse your credit cards in the first place! If you have several credit cards, that's several too many. Cut all of them up except one and only use that for emergencies, like car repairs while traveling or for unforeseen medical expenses. Otherwise, put the card away (and watch your disposable income pile up each month).

Knute's Knotes

Credit Card Counselors

If you've got so much credit card debt that you can't sleep at night, you might want to seek some legitimate professional financial help. One of the best organizations at helping consumers pare down their credit card debt is the National Foundation for Consumer Credit (NFCC). According to NFCC President Durant Abernathy, NFCC counselors can help debt-impaired individuals create a financial plan that will eliminate that debt in time. They'll help you set financial priorities, establish a budget, and identify action steps to help you achieve your financial goals. Give them a call at 800-388-2227. Spanish-speaking counselors can be reached at 800-682-9832.

After all, do you really need that $800 mountain bike? Immediate gratification is the bane of the American consumer. If you want the mountain bike that badly, save for it over time and pay with cash. You'll appreciate it more and your budget won't suffer.

The one credit card you keep should be chosen carefully. The banks that issue these cards don't all charge the same interest rate and don't all abide by the same fee rules. Just because you have a VISA card, that doesn't mean that it offers the same interest rates as the VISA your brother uses.

It's a good idea to compare interest rates between cards both at the start of your card agreement and over the long haul. How often do the rates change? Is there a "grace period" on new purchases or does the credit card issuer smack you with interest fees right away after a new purchase? Some don't. Call five banks you like and find out who offers the best deals (the rates can change as often as daily). Two organizations, CardTrak (800-334-7714) and Consumer Credit Card Rating Service (310-392-7720), have long-standing reputations for publishing reliable bank credit card information and rates. Call them.

In addition, look for cash-back rewards, frequent flyer milers, and other perks with your credit card. Don't be ruled by these perks—they're not as important as the interest rates you'll pay—but if you can swing a deal for a credit card with a reasonable interest rate package and, say, a good frequent-flyer offer to boot, so much the better.

One last thing on paying down debt. Before you cut anyone a check, make sure you see a copy of your credit report. Businesses report your financial activities to credit-reporting companies who in turn issue regular "state-of-your-financial-health" documents to anyone who asks. Businesses, often retail stores and banks, review the reports to determine whether you're a safe risk for a department store credit card or mortgage loan. Unfortunately, it's not uncommon for the credit report issuers to err in their findings, or fail to give you a chance to tell your side of the story. Sometimes an unpaid phone bill is the result of a bookkeeping error, or an unpaid rent check simply the mistake of your old landlord. These bits of misinformation, left uncorrected, can needlessly damage your credit rating. By reviewing your credit report annually, you can nip headaches like that in the bud.

Knute's Knotes

The auto industry's Big Three—General Motors, Ford, and Chrysler—have nothing on the credit reporting biz. Three major credit bureaus comprise the bulk of the credit reporting industry. Call or write these companies to obtain a copy of your credit report or to report an error. Expect a fee of about $20.00 for a copy of your report.

1. Equifax Credit Information Services: (800-685-1111) P.O. Box 740241, Atlanta, GA 30374-0241. (Ask about their free brochures on consumer rights and about recent government laws on fair credit reporting activities.)
2. Trans Union Corporation (National Consumer Relations Disclosure Center): (312-258-1717) 25249 Country Club Blvd., North Olmsted, OH 44070.
3. TRW Information Services: (800-422-4879) 505 City Parkway West, Orange, CA 92668.

What Do You Need to
Live on in Retirement?

One of the great ironies of the modern age is the high level of insecurity Americans feel, even as the Great Economic Boom of the 1990s rolls on. According to a 1998 study released by the Employee Benefits Research Institute, only one-quarter of all working Americans surveyed said they would have enough money to retire comfortably. Asked to

Knute's Knotes

Credit Card Counselors II

On the one hand, credit card companies sometimes pursue unethical practices, such as issuing credit cards to heavy-using consumers who can't find the off switch on their MasterCards. On the other hand, the credit card industry has sponsored an organization dedicated to wiping out credit card addiction. Consumer Credit Counseling (800-388-2227) can help wean you off your credit card, set up a payment plan if you're in debt, and even offer tips on developing and maintaining a household budget.

project 20 years forward, virtually every survey respondent reported feeling "more worried" about meeting specific retirement costs in the year 2018.

The number of people surveyed who said they were doing a "good job" saving for their Golden Years dropped 7 percent from a similar 1997 survey, from 32 percent to 25 percent. Worse, the number of respondents who thought personal savings would be an "important source" of retirement income fell from 51 percent to 39 percent in the same time period.

No need to beat yourself over it, though. If you follow my lead and prepare a budget, climb out of debt, calculate your retirement needs now, and begin shoveling money away into your 401(k), your financial problems will be few and far between. Nobody wants to be poor when they get old, and the best way to prevent that is to prepare to get wealthy instead.

Knute's Knotes

Woes "R" Us

Americans are a gloom-and-doom lot when it comes to projecting their lives in retirement. Check out some additional findings from the 1998 Employee Benefits Research Institute Sixth Annual Retirement Confidence Survey:

- Thirty percent don't think they will have enough money to support themselves in retirement no matter how long they live.
- Half worry they won't have enough money for long-term health care.
- Almost one-third don't save anything, and half of those people said they had too many immediate financial responsibilities to do so.
- Twenty percent of retirees said their overall standard of living was worse than expected.
- Among ethnic groups, Asian Americans had the highest percentage of people who were very confident about having enough money to last through retirement (27 percent), while only 13 percent of African Americans described themselves as very confident, the lowest percentage. Almost one-quarter of Latinos (23 percent) were very confident about having enough.

Fear was a major factor in saving. Savers cited "seeing people not prepare and struggle" and a sense of "time running out" as the two strongest motivators. But the survey also found that 81 percent of workers who received retirement-planning information from employers saved for retirement compared with 67 percent of those who received no information. And 56 percent of those who got employer information tried to figure out how much they would need to retire on, compared with 38 percent who received no information.

Source: Employee Benefits Research Institute.

The best way to begin to grow wealth is to take an inventory of not only your budget, which we discussed using our cash flow worksheet, but your net worth as well. How can you manage your financial resources until you figure out what they are?

Skeptical? Try this test. Ask a friend or a neighbor how much his new four-wheel drive vehicle cost. He'll puff up and proudly blurt out the exact price, right down to the last dime. Then ask him what his net worth is. He'll probably stammer something about not getting around to that yet and quickly turn the conversation back to his brand-new shiny sports vehicle.

Unless your neighbor plans on delivering pizzas with it, his new Blazer won't do him any long-term good—although it might be great for his emotional health now. He needs to take the time to lay the groundwork for his financial future. Who knows? Calculating his net worth might have shown him that he couldn't afford that new car right now. That's what a net worth analysis can do for you. It honestly, bluntly, and completely tells you what your financial standing is. Stuff you really need to know.

Your *net worth* is the amount of money you have left after all of your debts are paid. It's the difference between your "assets" (what you hold) and your "liabilities" (what you owe). Your assets typically include your checking and savings accounts and other cash-equivalent investments, individually owned stocks and bonds, mutual fund holdings, home and life insurance, collectibles (like family heirlooms or a stamp collection), and personal property (like cars, furniture, and clothing, but don't place too much emphasis on personal property—it depreciates in value and doesn't add up to much). Your liabilities typically include your unpaid monthly bills, your mortgages and home equity loans, consumer loans (like auto and college loans), and miscellaneous items like unpaid taxes.

Remember that some of the items you'll record, like clothing and transportation expenses, will be reduced when you retire. It's also probable (unless you got a late start buying your home or starting a family) that your mortgage will be paid off and your kids' college bills will be a memory. So cheer up: you've got a lot more to look forward to in retirement than you think.

Complete this worksheet to find out your net worth.

 ## Cash Flow Worksheet

ASSETS

Cash and Cash Equivalents

Savings account _____
Cash management account _____
Money market account _____
Credit union account _____
Certificates of deposit _____
Other _____

Stocks and Bonds

Stocks _____
Bonds _____
Mutual funds _____
Unit trusts _____
Fixed income securities _____
Options _____
Futures _____
Commodities _____
Other _____

Real Estate

Value of your home _____
Value of any vacation
    homes _____

Rental properties _____
Real estate partnerships _____
Other _____
Other investments _____
Partnerships _____
Oil and gas _____
Ownership in
    businesses _____
Other _____
Collectibles _____
Gold and silver _____
Art _____
Antiques _____
Coins and stamps _____
Other _____

Retirement Assets

IRA _____
Keogh _____
401(k) _____
Company pension plan _____
Profit sharing _____
Savings plan _____

Cash Flow Worksheet (continued)

Insurance		LIABILITIES	
Cash value of life insurance	_____	Home mortgage	_____
Surrender value of annuities	_____	Other mortgages	_____
		Other real estate debts	_____
		Automobile loans	_____
		Insurance payments	_____
Personal Property		Tuition loans	_____
Automobiles	_____	Credit card debt	_____
Boats	_____	Other installment debt	_____
Campers	_____	Credit lines	_____
Plane	_____	Income taxes	_____
Jewelry	_____	Property taxes	_____
Household furnishings	_____	Margin loans from brokers	_____
Other	_____	Miscellaneous debt	_____
Other	_____		
Other	_____	TOTAL LIABILITIES	_____
Other	_____		
		NET WORTH	
		Total Assets	_____
		Less Total Liabilities	_____
TOTAL ASSETS	_____	Net Worth	_____

What You Need to Live on in Retirement

The amount of money you'll need for retirement depends on your goals, wants, and needs. If you want to live pretty much as you do now, a general guideline is that you'll need 75 percent of your current income. But if you want to go see the pyramids, camp out on the Serengheti plain, or sample cuisine from the great restaurants of Paris in retirement, you'll need more. That also goes if you want to help out with your grandchildren's college tuition or try to join the PGA Senior Golf Tour. Those kinds of outlays will demand about 100 percent of your current income—or more—in retirement.

You'll also need to establish at what age you want to retire. If you're going to retire at age 55, you're going to need a lot more money than you would if you walk away at age 70. Keep in mind that the earlier you retire, the lower your Social Security benefits will be, the lower your

401(k) earnings will be, and the lower your current income will be, since you're not drawing a paycheck anymore. It's extremely difficult to retire early *if* you don't start saving early. Retiring early is something that takes years of planning, so maybe you need to just work on retiring well, not early.

Knute's Knotes

Don't count on Social Security too much for your retirement assets. U.S. Labor Department statistics indicate that Social Security will make up less than one-quarter of the average American's retirement income (company pensions, personal savings, and tax-deferred retirement plans comprise the rest). You will get a check from Uncle Sam each month in retirement for your contributions to Social Security. To find out how much you can expect to draw in Social Security in your postworking years, contact the Social Security Administration at (800) 772-1213. Ask for a copy of Form SSA-7004-PC-OPC (otherwise known as the *Request for Earnings and Benefit Estimate Statement*). Your local Social Security office will probably have these forms available.

Keep in mind that Americans are living longer than ever and that odds are you'll live 20 or even 30 years in retirement. Unless you want to stick your kids with your retirement bill—which may include a stint in a nursing home if you live into your 80s and 90s—then you'll want to estimate what you'll need to live on in retirement and forge a financial plan to meet that goal.

Thanks to good health, major advancements in medicine and technology, and generally favorable health habits, Americans are living longer than ever. Now the challenge is figuring out how to pay for the additional time before you head for your great reward. Here's how long middle-aged and elderly Americans can expect to live in retirement:

REMAINING LIFE EXPECTANCY FOR
AMERICANS, IN YEARS, AGE 50–70

Age	All	Male	Female
50	29.4	27.1	31.5
55	25.2	23.0	27.1
60	21.2	19.2	22.9
65	17.5	15.7	18.9
70	14.1	12.5	15.3
75	11.1	9.8	11.9
80	8.3	7.3	8.9
85	6.1	5.4	6.4

Source: *Monthly Vital Statistics Report*, Vol. 46, No. 1 Supplement, 1996.

You're going to need a lot of money to live as well as you want to in retirement, so let's start now in determining how much you'll need. Track the following steps:

1. Current gross annual income: $ _____
2. Minus: Amount of annual savings: _____
3. Subtotal: What you currently spend: _____
4. Times 75 percent: _____
5. Current standard of living (the amount you need to live on right now): _____
6. Times inflation factor (See table on p. 66.): _____
7. Estimated annual living expenses at retirement: $ _____

INFLATION TABLE

No. of Years Until Retirement	Factor	No. of Years Until Retirement	Factor
5	1.2	25	3.0
10	1.6	30	3.7
15	1.9	35	4.7
20	2.4	40	5.8

Here's an example: Mary McGuire has 20 years until retirement. Her annual income is $40,000.

1. Mary's annual income: $40,000
2. Minus: Mary's annual savings (including 401(k) and other investments): $4,000
3. Mary's subtotal (the amount Mary spends annually): $36,000
4. Mary multiplies her subtotal ($36,000) by 75 percent (the estimated amount of Mary's current income that she will need to live on in retirement, based on U.S. government calculations): $36,000 × .75 = $27,000
5. Mary multiplies the inflation factor based on her years to retirement (2.4 based on accompanying inflation table): $27,000 × 2.4 (based on 20 years until retirement)
6. Mary now has her estimated, inflation-adjusted annual retirement income figure: $27,000 × 2.4 = $64,800

When Mary retires in 20 years, she can roughly expect to need $64,500 annually to live on in retirement.

Remember that the rate of your retirement savings progress also greatly depends on the average annual returns from your investments. In the past few years, the stock market has returned an average of about 25 percent annually. Don't expect that every year but, according to Ibbotson Associates, a Chicago-based market-tracking firm, the stock market has averaged investment returns of 12 percent annually (as long as you stay invested in the market). That kind of return over 20 or 30 years would greatly enhance your retirement savings prospects, to say the least (see table below). Chapters 6 and 7 are devoted to showing you what the best investments are and how the stock market works.

What are we waiting for? Let's get to the fun part: mutual funds and the stock market.

THE INVESTMENT RETURN DILEMMA: HOW MUCH WILL YOU HAVE TO RETIRE ON AT AGE 65?

Average Annual Total Return (Percent)	Beginning Age/Investing $200 Monthly (Investments Made at the Beginning of the Month)			
	25	35	45	55
3	$ 185,675	$ 116,839	$ 65,825	$28,018
5	306,476	167,145	82,549	31,186
8	702,856	300,059	118,589	36,833
10	1,275,356	455,865	153,139	41,310
15	6,280,751	1,401,964	303,191	55,731

Knute's Knotes

There's another way to calculate your retirement needs, but you need access to the Internet to use it. Many financial services companies and investment magazines offer retirement planning calculators on their World Wide Web sites. Two of the best are www.familymoney.com and www.nbfunds.com (Neuberger Berman Funds).

Any mutual fund worth its salt has a full retirement planning calculator available on its Web site. If you're online, you have all the information you need about retirement projections at your fingertips.

A 401(k) Makeover

Name: Bob K.

Age: 39

Occupation: Beer distributor manager

Retirement Goal: Retire at age 65, maybe later if I don't have enough socked away for retirement. I'd like to buy my own tavern in my hometown of Boston, Massachusetts, and hire my son to manage it for me. He's young, but great with numbers.

401(k) Assets: $112,000

Portfolio: 60% Stable value fund
20% Conservative equity income
20% Equity index fund

Stocks: None

Comments: Thanks to my brother, who's in banking, I started investing in my 401(k) early. He also told me to get more aggressive with my 401(k) portfolio, but I'm squeamish about losing it all in the stock market. So I've remained kind of conservative with my retirement plan.

Knute Says

Bob, you're in great shape to get to your dream. I strongly believe in the "sleep factor" . . . if worrying about your investments keeps you up at night, it is too risky for you. But one of my five rules is to educate yourself. Learning more about the stock market and mutual funds may enable you to take a bit more risk and still feel comfortable. For now, though, I would suggest more diversification. Choose an international fund and put about 10 percent of your money into it. Take it from the stable value fund.

5

The biggest mistake you can make is to believe that you work for someone else.

—E. T. Olson

Waiter, I'm Ready to Order

To the uninitiated, Wall Street and its vast world of 11,000 mutual funds can be an intimidating place. In fact, there are more mutual funds than there are stocks on the New York Stock Exchange and NAS-DAQ combined—more than 11,000 compared to about 9,400 stocks.

It doesn't have to be intimidating, though. One way to maximize your 401(k) investment (and a huge factor in becoming a 401(k) millionaire) is understanding the investment products that comprise your 401(k).

Tracking the performance of mutual funds can be fun. That's not always the case with handling the other components of your finances, like paying bills and figuring out your taxes. But I've always enjoyed choosing and monitoring the funds I used for my 401(k) plan. In fact, I compare investing to the Indianapolis 500: the 401(k) is your race car, the stock market is your track, and the mutual funds are the fuel that makes your engine go. You're the driver and you've got a crew (the fund's manager and analysts) to keep you on track. Start your engines.

Get to Know Your Funds

Mutual funds are fairly easy to understand. What can be difficult is creating a blend, or allocation, of mutual funds that offers the best chances of reaching your financial goals. That discussion involves allocating your assets and gauging your tolerance to risk.

The reason I bring up topics like asset allocation and risk now is to warn you that the chances of understanding either, let alone putting them to good use, is negligible if you don't possess a bedrock understanding of what mutual funds are and how they work. So in this chapter we'll learn more about funds so that we can create 401(k) investment strategies using mutual funds in Chapter 6.

Knute's Knotes

The Money Train

A trillion dollars here and a trillion dollars there—pretty soon you're talking about real money.

The mutual fund industry is coming on like a freight train. Fund companies estimate that over $5 trillion will have been invested in mutual funds by the end of 1998. That's up from $4 trillion in 1997.

Considering that the first mutual funds were offered in 1926, it took the fund industry almost 70 years (1994) to reach the $2.5 trillion mark in assets. Since then, it has taken less than four years to double that figure.

Do you think that you and your 401(k) fund had anything to do with that growth? You betcha.

A Mutual Fund Primer

As of mid-1998, over 40 million Americans had invested in mutual funds. That's about one in every three Americans pouring the stunning total of $4 trillion into mutual funds. The balance of power between institutional investors—the banks, brokerages, and other businesses that invest in the financial markets—and individual investors—people like you, me, and the mailman—has begun to swing in our favor because of the average American's preference for mutual funds.

You may recall the October 1997 stock market dive when the market fell several hundred points. Many Wall Street observers compared it to a similar crash in October 1987, ten years earlier almost to the day, when the stock market dropped 500 points in one trading session. The difference between the two events was the commitment by individual investors to their mutual fund investments. In 1987, many mom-and-pop investors fled the stock market in terror, liquidating their fund shares in a panic. But ten years later, with a renewed emphasis on staying invested for the long-term and remaining disciplined, individual investors stayed cool and left their fund money alone, even as many of the big institutional investors ran scared and sold, sold, sold. Many traders and brokers credited the little investor for keeping the market stable during the October 1997 market correction (as well as in September 1998) when the big boys were losing their heads. It's an indicator of the growing power of individual mutual fund investors, many of whom invest in funds through their 401(k) plans, and signals an impressive departure from the stock market environment of yesteryear, run by the old-boy's network of bankers and financiers.

That metamorphosis is due to the growing popularity of mutual funds with average Americans. What is it about these investment vehicles that keeps us coming back for more?

The Top 8 Things You Need to Know About Mutual Funds

Mutual fund investing deserves a book of its own (and there are plenty of them available). For novice investors, the following eight points can give you a great head start:

1. *What is a mutual fund?* A mutual fund pools the money of many investors, or shareholders as you are known to the fund

companies, and invests the cash in a variety of vehicles, thus diversifying the shareholder's investment. Typically, those investments include stocks, bonds, and money market securities. Sometimes, funds offer all three in one package. The combination of stocks, bonds, or other securities and assets the fund owns is known as a portfolio.

The securities that comprise the fund are managed by a professional called a money manager or mutual fund manager. This person works for the company that offers the mutual fund, investing in individual stocks and bonds on behalf of the fund's shareholders. Each investor holds a certain number of "shares" in the fund, and is rewarded when the fund's value increases and penalized when the fund's value decreases.

Unlike certain other investments, like U.S. Treasury Bonds, mutual funds are not backed by the full faith and credit of the U.S. government, nor are they insured by any bank on your behalf. Even if you buy shares in a bank mutual fund, there's no guarantee that you'll make money. There's always the possibility of losing money.

2. *What are stocks, bonds, and money market securities?* A *common stock* is a security that represents an ownership interest in a corporation. Investors in common stocks can benefit in two ways: The company can pay cash dividends to its stockholders and the shares may increase in value through capital appreciation. Not all stocks pay cash dividends.

Stocks enable investors to share ownership (or equity) in a company by buying a small piece of it. The inherent risk is that the company (and your piece of it) may decrease rather than increase in value. Unlike bonds, stocks don't come with a guarantee that you'll earn money.

A *bond* is a debt security or IOU, usually issued by a corporation, government, or government agency. Bond investors seek current income and preservation of principal. In other words, they want to protect the money they already have and make a little more on the side. Bond prices will vary and are strongly affected by interest rate changes. As a rule, when interest rates

Knute's Knotes

Stocks are your best bet for beating inflation. Or any other investment criteria for that matter. That's because, over the long haul, no other investment comes close to providing as high a rate of return. Check out the following chart:

Unparalleled Performance, 1959–1995

The value of $1 invested in stocks, corporate bonds, government bonds, treasury bills, and inflation from January 1, 1959 through December 31, 1995:

Stocks—$39.33
Corporate bonds—$13.97
Government bonds—$12.74
Treasury bills—$8.41
Inflation—$5.23

Source: Ibbotson Associates.

go down, the price of bonds rise (because the higher interest-earning bonds on the market are in greater demand). Conversely, when interest rates go up, the price of bonds go down (because the lower interest rate-earning bonds on the market are in less demand).

Money market instruments, also known as cash, are short-term debt investments. In general, they earn less interest than most stocks and bonds, but are relatively safer than stocks and bonds. Money market mutual funds invest in U.S. Treasury bills, "jumbo" certificates of deposit, and other short-term interest-bearing securities. Normally, securities in money market funds are held only from 30 to 90 days. Money market returns earn more than bank passbook savings accounts but less than stocks and bonds. *One note of caution:* Although money market investments are not guaranteed by the federal government, I have yet to meet anyone who went belly up financially because of a money market fund. They're about as safe an investment as you can find.

3. *Why mutual funds?* Mutual funds provide an opportunity to invest in multiple stocks or bonds, thus spreading—or diversifying—your investment risk. They also provide you with the benefit of professional money management experience. Mutual funds take the responsibility of managing your money off your shoulders and place it on the shoulders of the fund company (specifically, the fund manager). Don't get me wrong—I don't advocate giving up responsibility for your finances. But mutual funds are a proven, cost-efficient way of investing in some of the top ideas by the best investment professionals in the financial services industry. I call that smart investing.

Assisted by a bevy of researchers, analysts, and economists, fund managers tap into the hottest companies and the fastest-growing stocks (at least, that's the idea). That enables managers to buy the stocks with the most potential while weeding out those stocks with the least potential.

Plus, since your fund's manager buys and sells huge amounts of securities at a time (more than you'd likely buy or sell in a lifetime), the costs associated with those trades (i.e., commissions and fees) are much lower than what you would pay on your own.

Although $1,000 minimum investments had been the norm in the mutual fund industry for the past several years, fund company attitudes are changing. With so many retail investors interested in participating in the mutual fund boom, fund companies are obliging them by significantly lowering the minimum investment. Today, anyone with $50 to invest can usually participate in the mutual fund game. In fact, the fund companies are lining up to take your money. That's good news for the average American. So, for the price three CDs or a couple of videotapes, you can become a mutual fund investor.

That said, fund managers aren't foolproof. Many lose money for their shareholders. Remember with mutual funds that the government isn't going to mail you a check to cover losses incurred from your fund investments. If you lose money in a fund, *it's not insured.*

And unlike individual stock investors, you don't gain the full benefits of a major run-up by a company. When Pfizer Inc. released Viagra, the impotence-fighting drug, to great success, the company's stock price almost doubled in a matter of weeks. That's great news for owners of the stock, who saw their investment in Pfizer return almost 100 percent during that time. But mutual fund shareholders whose funds held Pfizer stock didn't fare as well. While the fund's performance was no doubt boosted by Pfizer, the company was one of only 30, 40, or even 50 stocks that the mutual fund might have held.

If Pfizer suffered bad economic news and its stock price suffered as a result, the company's stockholders would suffer significantly. Pfizer's negative impact on a mutual fund, however, would likely be blunted by the performance of the other stocks in the portfolio, most of which would have nothing to do with Pfizer or Viagra. That's why fund managers like to diversify, especially in different industries. Downturns in one sector are usually offset by upturns in another.

4. *What's this diversification I keep hearing about?* Diversification means dividing your investments among more than one type of "vehicle." It's one of the best ways, if not *the* best way, to protect your portfolio from the pendulum swings of the economy and the financial markets. Since a mutual fund may invest in hundreds or even thousands of different securities, a decline in the value of one security may be offset by the rise in value of another.

If you attempted to build your own diversified investment portfolio of 50 stocks, you'd likely wind up paying tens of thousands of dollars in trading commission charges for the privilege.

A mutual fund enables you to get that kind of diversified investment but with a reasonable management fee.

Put it this way: Rather than using 30 grocery carts to tote each of your individual groceries around, you use one cart. Simple, right? Well, mutual fund diversification works much the same way. Instead of having a dozen different portfolios holding one security each, a mutual fund allows you to place multiple securities into one "basket." Now doesn't that make things easier all around?

Knute's Knotes

Spreading the Wealth Around

Diversification means your investment results don't depend on any single investment. Check out the difference between investing $100,000 in one lump sum and investing $100,000 in five separate $20,000 increments:

$100,000 Among 5 Investment Choices

Inv 1	Inv 2	Inv 3	Inv 4	Inv 5
$20K at a complete loss = $0	$20K at 0% return = $20K	$20K at 8% return = $93,219	$20K at 10% return =$134,550	$20K at 15% return = $327,331

After 20 years total diversified investment	= $575,100
$100,000 lump sum investment (earning 8% interest) after 20 years	= 466,096
Difference earned through diversification	= $109,004

5. *How can I invest in a mutual fund?* Easily. Mutual funds issue shares of stock in exchange for cash. Specifically, your cash. The money deducted from your 401(k) plan every paycheck is earmarked for the mutual fund or funds you've selected for your investment portfolio.

Knute's Knotes

I tend to do most of my reading in bits and pieces, riding on the train, waiting in the doctor's office, and so on. So most of my research is done via the printed page—magazines, newsletters, or a newspaper that I can roll up and put in my back pocket. But there's nothing like the Internet for getting information. Try these great Web sites as your first step. They offer you links to thousands of other fund-related Web sites:

- Mutual Fund Cafe (www.mfcafe.com): Performance data on thousands of mutual funds, plus chat rooms, bylined articles from leading financial journalists, and plenty of other good stuff.
- Mutual Fund Investor's Center (www.mfea.com): Similar to Mutual Fund Cafe, it offers great fund performance tracking, lively discussions, and some good research material.
- CNN Financial (www.cnnfn.com): A little broader in scope than the Mutual Fund Cafe and the Mutual Fund Investor's Center, CNN Financial offers helpful advice and research on other financial topics, like investing in individual stocks and how to minimize your tax bill.
- DejaNews (www.dejanews.com): Click on "business/money," then click on "investments" and then click on "mutual funds." Right before your eyes appears an index of 2,162 mutual fund Web pages. Happy hunting!
- The Investor Education Network (www.investoreducation.org): Great data on risk and return, asset allocation, and other fund investment criteria. Lots of interactive worksheets to calculate fund performance and retirement planning needs.

Once you select your mutual fund, a prospectus or description of the fund is mailed to you by the fund provider. A prospectus is a legal document required by the Securities and Exchange Commission (SEC)—the government agency that monitors the mutual fund industry—that describes your fund in detail. It usually includes recent fund performance, fees and expenses, fund holdings, the fund's investment objective, and a list of fund managers and possibly the fund's board of directors. After a thorough review of the prospectus, you fill out an application and provide instructions to your employee benefits manager regarding your bank, your checking account number, and how the money is to be deducted (in the case of a 401(k) plan, the money is usually deducted from each paycheck).

Mutual funds are bought and sold based on a performance benchmark known as net asset value (NAV). NAV is the fund company's best guess of the value of a share of the fund (i.e., the value of the fund's underlying securities). It's also used in newspapers as a de facto current price of buying and selling the fund. How is the NAV calculated? The process is not as complicated as you might think. The fund companies take the daily closing price of all securities held by the fund, subtract some of that amount for liabilities, divide that result by the number of outstanding shares, and you have your NAV. That's the price per share, in dollars and cents, you would receive if you sold the shares that day.

Once you're a shareholder, you'll receive quarterly reports listing account activity, balances, and values. These reports detail all transactions, including purchases and sales of securities in the fund. Through your quarterly statements, you can track your fund's performance, although in most cases you can also track the fund's performance through your daily newspaper or via the Internet. Your 401(k) fund investments are usually updated daily, giving you instant access to your fund's current market value and share balances. Check with your employee benefits representative or your latest quarterly report from your fund company for a toll-free number you can use to check your fund's activity.

Knute's Knotes

You know what used to drive me batty? All those fund companies that claimed the objectives of their fund was "clearly stated" in their prospectuses. To whom, Albert Einstein? The assembly instructions for my new barbecue grill were easier to decipher—and they were half in French!

Fund prospectuses have historically been receptacles for bureaucratic jargon, questionable English, and financial gobbledegook, but not anymore. The Securities and Exchange Commission and the National Association of Securities Dealers have banded together to make financial services companies provide "clear-and-plain" prospectuses to investors. A survey by the Investment Company Institute, the mutual fund industry's trade group, found that only half of fund shareholders consulted a prospectus before making an investment. A separate survey by the SEC and the U.S. Comptroller of the Currency found investors viewed prospectuses as only the fifth best source of information.

By December 1, 1998, all mutual fund companies should have overhauled their fund prospectuses and made them easier to read. The profiles can be made available on the Internet, by mail, in newspapers, or in other media. Each prospectus was expected to run about 3 to 6 pages instead of the 20 or 30 pages of old.

In addition, the prospectuses themselves will have to be overhauled to provide clearer disclosure in plain English of mutual fund risks, fees charged to investors, and investment strategies and performance. Thank you, Uncle Sam.

6. *What are load and no-load funds and why should I care?* Load funds charge a fee, sometimes up to 9 percent of your assets annually, to manage and market the fund. The fee is called a "load." A mutual fund that charges no fees is called a no-load fund.

It's difficult to say which fund class is preferable. As a general rule, I like to keep my fund expenses down as much as possible. That's why I prefer no-load funds. Many Wall Streeters will tell you that the fees paid for load funds go into additional research staff, multiple fund managers, or other potential benefits.

But remember this: If you invest $10,000 in a no-load mutual fund and $10,000 in a load mutual fund with a 5 percent sales charge, there's a big difference. With the load fund, the fund company will take $500 right off the top (5 percent of $10,000). That leaves you with $9,500 to invest compared to the $10,000 that you'd have with a no-load fund.

7. *What's the downside of investing in mutual funds?* Not much that I can see. Often, fund companies, especially those that offer load funds, can charge what I consider to be exorbitant fund expenses that can really take the wind out of your portfolio's performance.

Also, unlike individual stocks and bonds where you can make your own selections, mutual funds put you at the mercy of another person's investment opinions (but then again, that's what you're paying your fund manager for).

Another factor is taxes. If you sell shares in a mutual fund for a profit, you must pay capital gains on that profit. Correspondingly, if you sell shares in a mutual fund that lost money you can gain some tax benefits from what are known as capital losses. Although Congress has loosened some of the capital gains restrictions incurred from selling shares in a mutual fund, capital gains taxes can still hurt in ways you least expect. (Formerly, 28 percent of the assets earned from the sale of an investment such as a stock, bond, or mutual fund were taxed as capital gains. That figure dropped to 20 percent in the 1997 Tax Reform Act, as long as the investment had been held for 12 months.) For example, the buying and selling of securities by the fund manager alone are taxable events, incurring capital

Knute's Knotes

Beware the "Fee-Only" Financial Advisor Bearing Fund Advice

I get on stockbrokers' cases sometimes, but I have to give them credit. At least when you're dealing with a broker, you know he's motivated by the potential commission from your business. Not always so with a financial advisor. Financial advisors make their living managing not just your investments but your retirement planning, estate planning, and other critical lifetime financial management needs. Most do so with impeccable honesty. In fact, financial advisors can take on not only your investment responsibilities but your personal budgeting and estate and tax planning as well. Many investors develop lifelong relationships with their financial advisors, trusting them to manage their money right through their retirement years.

But some bad apples do exist in the financial planning industry. Some of these folks call themselves "fee-only" planners—meaning they draw an annual fee for your financial planning needs, usually around 1 percent or 2 percent of your total assets. But if they talk you into a mutual fund that pays a load fee, watch out. Chances are they're getting a commission from the fund company off the top for the sale, in which case fee-only turns into "fee-and-commission, soak-the-client-only."

That's the trouble with load funds. Some financial planners have arrangements with mutual fund companies to market their load funds. Whether they perform well or not, you're always left wondering if the financial planner who sold you on the fund was looking out for your best interest or his.

gains or losses even if you sell no shares of the fund. Those gains or losses will show up on your annual fund shareholder tax statement and should be accounted for in your tax return.

8. *Okay, you've been raving about fund expenses for half the book, it seems. What are they?* Yes, I know I tend to go over the top on fund expenses. But that's only because it's my hard-earned money, and I want to see it go as far as possible.

Most mutual funds, both load and no-load, stick a price tag on the research and trading services they provide. Load funds go a step further—a big step further—by adding an annual fee of anywhere between 1 percent and 9 percent that is subtracted on the front end of the fund investment (when you pay the fund company before you invest—at the front end). These expenses are usually earmarked for commissions paid to brokers and financial advisors who sell you the fund. Keep that in mind the next time a broker calls you during dinner about the next hot fund. Ask him if he's willing to forgo his commission if the fund is so hot. Then listen to the dial tone as he hangs up.

How Many Different Kinds of Mutual Funds Are There?

To keep things plain and simple, only about a dozen or so fund classes warrant our interest. These are the primary mutual funds you'll likely find in your 401(k) plan menu. Because mutual funds each have specific investment objectives such as growth of capital, safety of principal, current income, or tax-exempt income, you can select one fund or any number of different funds to help you meet your specific goals:

- *Stock Funds.* These invest in common stocks. Stocks usually have higher short-term risk than bonds, but have historically produced the best long-term returns. Stock funds often hold small amounts of money market investments to meet redemptions; some hold larger amounts of money market investments when they cannot find any stock worth investing in or if they believe the market is about to head downward.

But that hardly begins to describe the many different kinds of stock funds. Here are the stock mutual funds that 401(k) plans normally provide:

- *Growth Stock Funds.* These funds, which can be volatile, seek maximum earnings potential and high share prices from the hard-charging companies they invest in. Growth funds invest in fast-growing, well-established companies where the company itself and the industry in which it operates are thought to have good long-term growth potential. A good example of a growth fund is Fidelity's Magellan Fund, which for years was the highest-returning mutual fund in the industry.
- *Aggressive Growth Funds.* Similar to growth funds, but these funds are even more aggressive; they tend to be the most volatile. Aggressive growth funds seek to provide maximum growth of capital with secondary emphasis on dividend or interest income. They invest in common stocks with a high potential for rapid growth and capital appreciation. That comes at no small risk: aggressive growth funds, since they bet on the fortunes of small, up-and-coming companies with little or no track record, are riskier than most funds. A good example of an aggressive growth fund is American Century's Ultra Fund, which blew away the competition in the early- to mid-1990s. In the last few years, though, Ultra has struggled because of its sustained exposure to so many high-risk companies.

Both traditional growth funds and aggressive growth funds are okay if you have a long time horizon before retiring. If you have 80 percent of your 401(k) assets in an aggressive growth fund at age 55, and the stock market tanks, you could lose a lot of your retirement money. But at age 25, 35, or even 45, aggressive growth funds are a good investment, since their returns typically outpace most other funds' performance.

Knute's Knotes

Growth Funds Rule: Since 1976, the average growth fund has outperformed the Standard & Poor 500 Index (the standard against which most stock funds are measured) by 600 percent!

- *Growth and Income Funds.* These funds seek both long-term growth and a reasonable amount of dividend income. Income stocks are those that have a history of paying high dividends. Generally an income stock operates in a fairly stable industry, like utilities. Income companies traditionally pay out a relatively high percentage of corporate earnings as dividends to common stock holders.

   Because the companies distribute rather than reinvest their profits, their stocks are less likely to grow as fast and high as more aggressive asset classes, like growth stocks. Income stocks are a good idea for conservative investors who need steady cash flow from their stock investments.

   Although fund management strategies vary among fund managers, two management strategies usually apply with growth and income funds: the funds invest in a dual portfolio consisting of growth stocks and income stocks, or a combination of growth stocks, stocks paying high dividends, preferred stocks, convertible securities or fixed-income securities such as corporate bonds and money market instruments.

   Growth and income funds are popular with fund investors, because they offer good opportunity for growth while also offering some protection against excessive risk.

- *International Stock Funds.* I love international funds, if only because my money gets to travel to more interesting places than I do. International funds focus on stocks of companies outside the United States. International funds are not to be confused with global funds, which seek growth by investing in securities around the world, including the United States. Both provide investors with another opportunity to diversify their mutual fund portfolio, since foreign markets do not always move in the same direction as the United States.

One caveat about international funds: they're not my first choice to park too much money in if you're close to retirement. International fund managers like to invest in overseas growth companies that operate under different rules and regulations and with different currencies than U.S. stocks. That doesn't mean foreign funds are not profitable. Actually they've proven quite durable over the past 10 years or so. But there is some added risk in sending a big chunk of your retirement money overseas when you're better off with a more conservative investment like a bond fund.

- *Stock Index Funds.* These funds attempt to mirror the performance of a specific market index, like the Standard and Poor 500 (which tracks Wall Street's top 500 stocks). Expenses are usually very low, typically below 1 percent of assets. Both the holdings and the performance should reflect the index the fund is trying to emulate.

- *Balanced Stock Funds.* By mixing stocks and bonds (and sometimes other types of assets), a balanced fund usually offers lower risk than investing in either alone, since different types of assets rise and fall at different times. Generally these funds have three objectives: to preserve investors' investment principal; to pay high current income through dividends and interest; and to promote long-term growth of both principle and interest.

- *Fixed-Income Funds.* More informally known as bond funds, fixed income funds attempt to provide high current income while preserving investors' money. Growth of capital, the hallmark of most stock funds, is of secondary importance to bond funds. Unlike stock funds, bond funds invest in securities that offer "fixed" rates of return. That means that you pretty much know what you're going to get on the return from your investment.

Knute's Knotes

Mutual funds can hold anywhere between 10 and 3,000 securities. On average, though, they hold 50 securities.

Now think about that: Where else can you go to invest in 50 hand-picked stocks or bonds selected by a highly trained financial specialist? Who else but a fund company will send you a statement every quarter detailing the investment performance of the dozens of companies that comprise your fund—all on a single sheet of paper and with no trading commissions? That's why mutual funds are such a great deal.

The chief variable in a bond fund is its price. Since bond prices fluctuate with changing interest rates, there is some risk involved despite a bond fund's conservative nature. When interest rates rise, the market price of fixed-income securities declines and so will the value of the income funds' investments. Conversely, in periods of declining interest rates, the value of fixed-income funds will rise and investors will enjoy capital appreciation as well as income. That's because in a declining interest rate environment, existing bonds that offer higher fixed rates of return are in greater demand. When rates rise, bonds that lock returns in at lower interest rates are in lower demand.

I consider bond funds to be "sandwich" investments: wedged between higher earning, higher risk stock funds and lower earning, lower risk money market funds (described next). Certain bond funds are an exception. High-yield, or "junk" bonds—the ones that gave Wall Street a black eye in the mid-1980s, thanks to high-rollers like Michael Milken and Ivan Boesky who went to jail for illegal bond trading activities—carry more risk than many traditional growth stock funds.

Other fixed-income funds seek to minimize risk by investing exclusively in securities whose timely payment of interest and principal is backed by the full faith and credit of the U.S. government. These include securities issued by the U.S. Treasury, the Government National Mortgage Association (Ginnie Mae securities), the Federal National Mortgage Association (Fannie Maes), and Federal Home Loan Mortgage Corporation (Freddie Macs). Government funds invest only in national government or government agency debt. They have slightly lower credit risk than regular bond funds. Treasury funds invest only in direct obligations of the national government. U.S. Treasury Bond funds offer investors the lowest credit risk, and dividend distributions are exempt from state income taxes in most states. They're great investments for 401(k) investors who are drawing near to retirement.

- *Municipal Bond Funds.* This is another bond-oriented investment I like. Municipal bond funds invest only in the debt of state or local governments, which use the bonds to raise money for civic projects, like new roads and bridges. For most individuals, dividend distributions from these bond funds are also exempt from national income taxes, and some are exempt from state and local taxes as well. But because of the tax-deferred status of the 401(k) plan, these bond funds should not be part of your 401(k) or IRA portfolios.
- *Money Market Funds.* The safest of all mutual funds, money market funds try to maintain a constant value per share, while yielding dividends from their investments in short-term debt securities. They invest in highly liquid, virtually risk-free, short-term debt securities of agencies of the U.S. government, banks and corporations, and U.S. Treasury Bills. They have no potential for growth. Their market value is also not insured by the FDIC or other government agency. Enough defaults in the fund's securities can cause it to be unable to maintain its constant value, though that's a highly unlikely prospect.

Knute's Knotes

The Straight Skinny on Money Market Funds

Money market funds are as close as you can get to your bank savings account, only with better returns. Money market funds offer yields that are usually somewhat higher than yields on bank certificates of deposit (CDs) as well. They also compare favorably with bank CDs in other areas:

1. Money can be withdrawn from a money market fund at any time without penalty. CDs, on the other hand, require money to be kept on deposit for a fixed period of time and impose penalties for early withdrawal.
2. Money market funds usually offer check-writing privileges.
3. Money market funds are suitable for conservative investors who choose safety over returns and want immediate access to their money.

What Are Some of the Better-Performing Mutual Funds?

The top mutual fund performers for the past one, three, and five years, as of April 30, 1998 are listed in the following table.

TOP 5-YEAR FUND PERFORMANCE

Fund	1 Year	3 Year	5 Year
1. Fidelity Select Electronics	25.10%	34.09%	35.65%
2. Seligman Communications & Information A	44.03	23.28	34.01
3. Fidelity Select Home Finance	54.69	42.74	33.21
4. Seligman Communications & Information D	42.88	22.33	32.50
5. Fidelity Select Computers	31.35	27.48	31.96
6. Weitz Hickory	85.76	49.82	31.03
7. Fidelity Select Health Care	45.25	32.46	30.10
8. Legg Mason Value Prim	49.15	42.52	29.61
9. Alliance Technology A	41.15	24.84	29.56
10. Safeco Growth No Load	89.37	40.03	29.34

TOP 10-YEAR FUND PERFORMANCE

	1 Year	3 Year	5 Year	10 Year
1. Fidelity Select Home Finance	54.69%	42.74%	33.21%	28.09%
2. Fidelity Select Regional Banks	49.06	41.99	27.97	26.15
3. Invesco Strategic Financial Services	51.40	40.14	25.06	25.75
4. Kaufmann Fund	36.11	24.25	22.00	25.13
5. Seligman Communications & Information A	44.03	23.28	34.01	24.96
6. John Hancock Regional Bank B	51.84	39.34	27.80	24.92
7. Fidelity Select Health Care	45.25	32.46	30.10	24.45
8. Invesco Strategic Health Sciences	40.47	29.98	24.24	24.44
9. Fidelity Select Electronics	25.10	34.09	36.65	24.31
10. Chase Vista Growth & Income A	37.97	26.43	18.09	24.00

Source: Morningstar, Inc. Last updated April 30, 1998.

Knute's Knotes

Quick Tip: Ask your mutual fund provider whether the portfolio managers and other executives of the firm have invested money in the fund.

I prefer knowing that my fund company has the same personal commitment to the success of the fund that I have. That's why I like the Vanguard Funds. Company founder John Bogle puts his money where his mouth is: He has about $35 million of his own money socked away in his company's funds.

A 401(k) Makeover

Name: Kristin D.

Age: 23

Occupation: Florist

Retirement Goals: I want to own my own flower shop one day, whether I can retire early to do that I don't know. But I'd like to plan my retirement so that if I make $1 million in my 401(k), I can retire right away no matter how old I am at the time.

401(k): $6,780

Portfolio: 30% Long-term stable value fund
25% Large-cap growth fund
15% Mid-cap value fund
10% Growth-and-income fund
10% Small-cap aggressive growth
10% International equity fund

Stocks: None

Comments: I had my mom and dad help choose my 401(k) investments, because I really don't know much about money. But I'm willing to learn!

Knute Says

You have two huge advantages going for you—time and a willingness to learn. When I was your age I wasn't even a "thousandaire" yet and you've got me beat by at least 6 times over! Now about your portfolio. Diversity is good but you're overdoing a good thing. You have less than $7,000 divided among 6 funds—way too many. Three of those funds have less than $700! Divide your money into two funds—a large cap growth fund and a small cap agressive growth. When your assets grow to more than $10,000, add additional money to another fund, perhaps a midcap value fund. And remember the rules: Start early, max out, educate yourself, be aggressive, and don't withdraw.

6

> *Doubt is often the beginning of wisdom.*
>
> *—M. Scott Peck*

The Risk Factor: An Investment Strategy to Help You Sleep Better at Night

If, after you launch your 401(k) into the turbulent waters of the financial markets, you find yourself lying wide awake at night, paralyzed with fear and chewing your pillow over the fact that the stock market fell 100 points the day before, you may want to adjust your portfolio.

To avoid sleepless nights, it's imperative that you build a 401(k) investment portfolio that is comfortable for you, that fits your investment risk parameters, and that leaves you ample room for investment growth. You should also pin down just how much investment risk you can tolerate, taking into consideration time horizons, personal lifestyle, and your attitudes about money. Once you've taken those steps, you must then diversify your portfolio (also known as "asset allocation") so that returns from one type of investment can offset losses in another.

Examining your risk profile is a healthy and wise move for any investor, particularly when the risk profile revealed is augmented by a compatible asset allocation plan. There'll be no need to lose sleep over an investment portfolio you've built yourself.

It's 11:00 p.m. Do You Know What Your 401(k) Is Doing?

In Chapter 2 we touched upon the millions of Americans who are taking control of their financial future through their 401(k) plans. That is a double-edged sword. Sure, it's great to see Americans getting more involved with their money. After all, nobody has a more vested interest in your financial future than you and your family.

But paired with the responsibility that came with the transition from the company-funded pension to the era of the 401(k) was an obligation to choose wisely when investing our retirement plan proceeds. Today, in exchange for gaining full ownership rights to our retirement money—something we didn't have with a company-funded pension plan—Americans now carry the weight of deciding how much money to save, what assets should be included in our 401(k) plans, and who will manage our money.

That autonomy, that freedom, that responsibility to take control of our financial lives is what makes investment risk such a big issue these days. It's no secret that investment risk has felled investors larger than you or I. On a large scale, investment risk was the culprit when Orange County, California, officials lost $1.7 billion of investors' money by betting the wrong way on interest rates. Investment risk was at the center of the UK-based Barings Bank debacle in 1995, when a rogue trader based in Singapore cost the internationally known bank billions in bad trades, nearly bankrupting the centuries-old financial institution. On an individual basis, all through their working years, investors face the risk of investing too conservatively—and thus not outpacing inflation—or investing too aggressively in high-risk ventures like real estate—and jeopardizing their financial futures.

Taking on too much—or not taking on enough—investment risk can topple your carefully planned 401(k) plan like a house of cards in a hurricane, slowing investment gains and reducing your chances of becoming a 401(k) millionaire. Even small differences in investment returns, when compounded over time, can have a tremendous effect on the amount of money you will have during retirement.

Knute's Knotes

The Downside of Not Taking Enough Risk

Money market funds are considered relatively stable because of their low-risk, shorter bond maturities. When your investment matures in 30, 60, or 90 days, there's little chance of losing much money.

In most financial circles, money market funds are considered "safe" investments. Are they? Money market returns historically have only been slightly higher than the rate of inflation, and far less than the long-term performance of stocks and bonds:

Comparative Returns from 12/31/25 through 12/31/97:

Small Company Stocks	12.71%
Stocks (S&P 500 Index)	11.00
Bonds	5.26
Bills	3.76
CPI	3.10

Source: Ibbotson Associates.

In this context, "safe" is a curious description of money market funds: They're poor choices as the sole component of your 401(k) portfolio. They're much better suited for parking your money for short-term needs, like the months before you buy a house, start paying college tuition, or spring for a new car. But not for your long-term retirement needs.

Risky Business

The trade-off between risk and reward cannot be over-emphasized. The more uncertain the investment, the greater the investment risk. The greater the investment risk, the greater the opportunity for hefty investment returns. If you're uncomfortable with too much risk and seek to minimize it, then you'll be penalized with lower investment returns. One thing's for sure, *you can't completely eliminate risk*. And if you don't take any risk, you surely won't make any money.

Investment risk is perpetually tied to market volatility—the fluctuations in the financial markets that constantly appear over time. The sources of this volatility are many: interest rate changes, inflation, political consequences, and economic trends all can create combustible market conditions that can change a portfolio's performance results in a hurry. Ironically, it is the very nature of this volatility that creates the opportunities for economic benefit in our 401(k) portfolios. Volatility often works in the investor's favor, as it has during the bull market of the mid- to late 1990s.

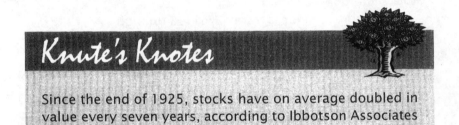

Knute's Knotes

Since the end of 1925, stocks have on average doubled in value every seven years, according to Ibbotson Associates in Chicago, a financial research firm.

What's Your Tolerance for Risk?

How much risk you can take depends on many factors: your age, your financial needs, your comfort level, how many dependents you have. If you're 25 years old, single, childless, and debt-free, you obviously have way more tolerance for risk than a 55-year-old nearing retirement with two kids in college.

Knute's Worksheet

Gauge Your Tolerance for Risk

Trying to pin down your tolerance for risk is akin to chasing ghosts: It's an uncertain process that's forever susceptible to second-guessing. You can never be quite sure what your tolerance for risk will be from year to year. But this test, can help clear things up. (Answers are on p. 99.)

1. If someone made me an offer to invest 15 percent of my net worth in a deal he said had an 80 percent chance of being profitable, I'd say:
   A. No level of profit would be worth that kind of risk.
   B. The level of profit would have to be seven times the amount I invested.
   C. The level of profit would have to be three times the amount I invested.
   D. The level of profit would have to be at least as much as my original investment.

2. How comfortable would I be assuming a $10,000 debt in the hope of achieving a $20,000 gain over the next few months?
   A. Totally uncomfortable. I'd never do it.
   B. Somewhat uncomfortable. I'd probably never do it.
   C. Somewhat uncomfortable. But I might do it.
   D. Very comfortable. I'd definitely do it.

3. I am holding a lottery ticket that's gotten me to the finals, where I have a 1 in 4 chance of winning the $100,000 jackpot. I'd be willing to sell my ticket before the drawing, but for nothing less than:
   A. $15,000   C. $35,000
   B. $20,000   D. $60,000

4. How often do I bet more than $150 on one or more of these activities: professional sports gambling, casino gambling, or lottery tickets?

A. Never.

B. Only a few times in my life.

C. Just in one of these activities in the past year.

D. In two or more of these activities in the past year.

5. If a stock I bought doubled in the year after I bought it, I'd:

A. Sell all my shares.

B. Sell half my shares.

C. Not sell any shares.

D. Buy more shares.

6. I have a high-yielding certificate of deposit that is about to mature, and interest rates have dropped so much that I feel compelled to invest in something with a higher yield. The most likely place I'd invest the money is:

A. U.S. savings bonds.

B. A short-term bond fund.

C. A long-term bond fund.

D. A stock fund.

7. Whenever I have to decide where to invest a large amount of money, I:

A. Delay the decision.

B. Get someone else, like my broker, to decide for me.

C. Share the decision with my advisers.

D. Decide on my own.

8. Which of the following describes how I make my investment decisions?

A. Never on my own.

B. Sometimes on my own.

C. Often on my own.

D. Totally on my own.

9. My luck in investing is:
A. Terrible.
B. Average.
C. Better than average.
D. Fantastic.

10. My investments are successful mainly because:
A. Fate is always on my side.
B. I was in the right place at the right time.
C. When opportunities arose, I took advantage of them.
D. I carefully planned them to work out that way.

Grading: Give yourself one point for each answer A, two points for each answer B, three points for each answer C, and four points for each answer D.

Results: *19 points or fewer:* You're a conservative investor who feels uncomfortable taking risks. You probably realize that you will have to take some calculated risks to attain your financial goals, but this doesn't mean you will be comfortable doing so.

20 to 29 points: You're a moderate investor who feels comfortable taking moderate risks. You are probably willing to take reasonable risks without a great deal of discomfort.

30 or more points: You're an aggressive investor who is willing to take high risks in search of high returns. You are not greatly stressed by taking significant risks.

Source: Lincoln Benefit Life, a subsidiary of Allstate Life Group.

The Different Types of Risk

There's no shortage of risk classes. Some are more complicated than others. Not all of the more complex ones are listed here, but the ones we'll discuss next are the primary forms of risk you'll likely run into when investing in your 401(k) plan.

Risk of Losing Your Money

The most formidable element of risk you face as an investor is the risk of losing some or all of your money. That was the case in October 1987 when the stock market fell 500 points—losing 22.5 percent of its value in a single day. In that instance, the value of a $10,000 investment in the stock market would have fallen to $7,740.

Mutual funds, by their diversified nature, severely diminish your chances of losing a lot of money. Whereas an investor dabbling in individual stocks can see his investment wiped out, the chances of that happening in a mutual fund are remote, if not extinct. Funds normally invest in about 50 companies. The chances of all 50 companies going broke at the same time are slim indeed.

Risk of Passivity

I know some perfectly reasonable people who don't trust the financial markets and who feel more comfortable sticking their money in a bank savings account. Big mistake.

Here's why: by sticking $10,000 in your bank savings account and being "passive" with your money, that is, not accepting the risks and rewards that go with investing in the stock market, you will wind up losing money. Passbook savings account interest currently amounts to about 2.5 percent, not even enough to keep up with the 3.4 percent rate of inflation. So your initial $10,000 actually decreases its purchasing power the longer it stays in your savings account.

Inflation Rate Risk

A blood brother of passivity risk, inflation risk is based upon the purchasing power of a dollar down the road. What we can purchase for $10,000 today will cost us $13,440 in the year 2008, based on 3 percent annual growth in inflation. Typically, stock funds are the best 401(k) investment when looking to outpace inflation, and money market funds the least effective in combating inflation (see accompanying chart on growth stocks vs. S&P 500).

THE BENEFITS OF BEING AGGRESSIVE: AVERAGE ANNUAL RETURNS OF GROWTH FUND COMPARED TO THE S&P 500 INDEX; 1975–1996

Year	Growth Fund	vs.	S&P 500
75	38.57%		31.55%
76	24.23		23.64
77	2.82		−7.44
78	14.68		6.40
79	31.53		18.30
80	36.75		32.22
81	−1.49		−5.08
82	27.41		21.46
83	21.42		22.47
84	−1.18		6.27
85	29.22		31.74
86	15.32		18.69
87	3.79		5.26
88	14.77		16.61
89	27.25		31.68
90	−4.74		−3.12
91	37.23		30.48
92	8.69		7.62
93	11.95		10.06
94	−1.75		1.32
95	30.99		37.53
96	19.79		22.95
Annualized	16.79%		15.62%
Growth of $10K	$304,478.11		243,664.66

Source: Sage/America Online.

Amateur Hour?

According to *Wall Street Journal* columnist Holman W. Jenkins, a woefully common misapprehension is that adults in positions of authority know what they are doing. In politics we correct this with elections and in business with the stock market.

That's why when it comes to market risk, you should try not to put too much faith in what the so-called professionals have to say.

A recent study by Wilshire Associates, a Santa Monica, California-based financial consulting firm, estimates that regular investors could have earned an average 280.6 percent over the past 10 years following the asset-allocation advice of broker-house specialists.

But left to our own devices, we could have done even better! According to the study, investors could have earned 286 percent simply by buying and holding a portfolio of 55 percent stocks, 35 percent bonds, and 10 percent money market investments. (By themselves, money markets may not be a good investment, but a 10 percent stake protects some of your money from a market crash.)

One other thing. The 280 percent earned from the market experts comes with strings attached—fees, commissions, and other expenses that would have dragged that performance down even more.

Market Risk

Every time you invest money in the financial markets, even via a conservative money market mutual fund, you're subjecting your money to risk. With market risk, uncertainty due to changes in the overall stock market is caused by political, social, or economic events and the mood of the investing public.

Perhaps the biggest investment risk of all, though, is *not* subjecting your money to market risk. If you don't put your money to work in the stock market, you're unable to benefit from the stock market's consistent growth over the years.

Credit Risk

Usually associated with bond investments, credit risk is the possibility that a company, agency, or municipality might not be able to make interest or principal payments on its notes or bonds. The greatest risk of default is usually with corporate debt—companies go out of business all the time. There's no credit risk with Treasury-related securities, because they're backed by the full faith and credit of the U.S. government. To measure the financial health of bonds, credit agencies like Moody's and Standard & Poor's assign them investment grades. A-rated bonds are considered solid, while C-rated bonds are considered unstable.

Currency Risk

Normally related to international or emerging-market investing, currency risk is due to currency fluctuations that may affect the value of foreign investments or profits.

Interest Rate Risk

When bond interest rates rise, the price of the bonds falls (and vice versa). Fluctuating interest rates impact stocks and bonds in significant ways. Typically, the longer the maturity of the bond, the larger the impact of interest rate risk. But long-term bonds normally pay out higher yields to compensate for the greater risk.

Economic Risk

When the economy slows, corporate profits—and thus stocks—could be hurt. For example, political instability in the Middle East makes investing there a dicey deal at best, even though much of the region is flush with oil, arguably the world's most in-demand commodity. A war there, such as the Gulf War of 1990, can negatively impact the fortunes of companies that do business with countries like Saudi Arabia, Israel, or Syria.

Knute's Knotes

Risk Evaluation Resources

Here are some reference materials that can help you find your own risk comfort level:
1. "Understanding and Managing Risk," a free 12-page brochure available from the Mutual Fund Forum. Call (800) 200-1819.
2. The Investment Company Institute, a trade group for mutual funds, offers two nearly free brochures that discuss risk: "An Investor's Guide to Reading the Mutual Fund Prospectus" and "Eight Basics of Bond Fund Investing." For copies, write 1401 H St. N.W., Suite 1200, Washington, D.C., 20005-2148.

Using Asset Allocation to Manage Risk

Of the three major investment classes—stocks, bonds, and money market securities—stocks usually pose the greatest risk, bonds the second greatest risk, and money markets the least risk. Returns from the three investment classes are reversed, with stocks offering the best chance of investment gain, bonds the second best chance, and money markets the least chance for gains.

In the stock market's worst year, according to *The Los Angeles Times*, the value of big-company stocks fell 43.3 percent. In its best year, big company stocks rose 53.9 percent. There's no shortage of volatility—or good returns—in stocks. The returns of small company stocks, which are more volatile than big company stocks, have varied by as much as 78 percent in a given decade, whereas the returns on Treasury Bills (T-Bills) have varied by less than 1 percent. T-Bills are a sure bet, but the returns on that bet are thin.

In fact, $1 invested in big company stocks in 1926 would have earned you $1,114 by the end of 1995, even though big stocks lost money in 20 of those 70 years. Conversely, if you had invested $1 in Treasury Bills in the same period (with only one down year with minuscule losses), you would have earned only $12.87.

That's why creating a risk profile for yourself is critical to your financial fortunes. Some investors can go about their business knowing their 401(k)s are invested in higher risk funds like international and aggressive growth funds. Others can't, so they bulk up on conservative bonds funds. Whether you consider your investment philosophy to be aggressive, moderate, or conservative, you need to form an opinion of yourself as a risk investor and determine how you're going to feel about possibly losing 5 percent or 10 percent of your investment at certain times. Will you be all right with that? Or will it send you into a fit of sheer panic and have you pacing your bedroom floor at 4 A.M.?

Either way, a good asset allocation strategy can help. Maybe the reason why the calm investor can stay calm in a stock market fall is that she's cushioned her 401(k) portfolio with a sprinkling of bond and money market funds to augment the investments she's made in international and aggressive growth funds. And if you're the sort who can't sleep nights thinking about the stock market, liberal doses of Treasury or corporate bond funds to go along with your stock fund investments will protect you from wild market swings in the latter sector.

That's the premise of asset allocation. In the long run, it levels the playing field a bit without hurting your investment performance. In fact, most Wall Streeters now think that asset allocation is the

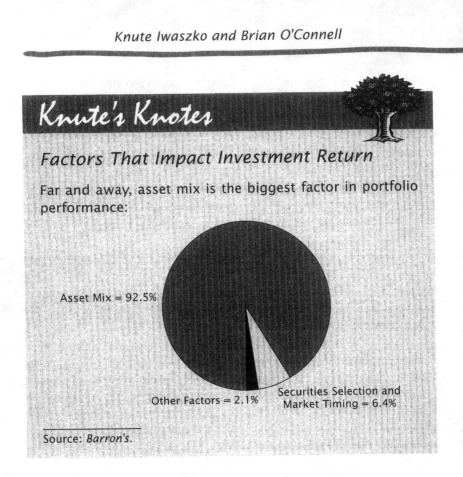

Knute's Knotes

Factors That Impact Investment Return

Far and away, asset mix is the biggest factor in portfolio performance:

Asset Mix = 92.5%

Other Factors = 2.1%

Securities Selection and Market Timing = 6.4%

Source: *Barron's*.

greatest factor in determining investment success—greater than security selection or other factors like market timing.

When you sprinkle a variety of mutual funds around your portfolio, you limit the possibility that any one fund can wipe out your portfolio. The following five steps can help frame your asset allocation strategy:

1. *Investment Goals:* The first step in the asset allocation process is something you've already done by now—determined how much money you're going to need for retirement and then estimated what kinds of investment returns you're going to need annually to reach those goals.

2. *Time Horizon:* Time horizon harkens back to the importance of starting early. If you started out your 401(k) plan at age 25, you're going to have a lot more time to weather the inevitable market declines. At age 50, your shorter time horizon calls for a more conservative risk outlook—you don't have the time to compensate for a 20 percent loss in your portfolio from a bear market.

3. *Attitudes About Risk:* Can you live with periodic market losses that can deplete your 401(k) by thousands of dollars at a time? If not, think more conservatively. If so, and you've got the time horizon in your favor, you can afford to think more aggressively.

4. *Financial Environment:* Have you created a budget? Do you have an emergency fund? Do you have big bills on the way, like a bigger mortgage or college costs? How close are you to retirement? Don't fool around with an aggressive investment portfolio if you're going to have to count on money soon. In short, your financial environment dictates what your asset allocation portfolio looks like. That's why things like budgeting and knowing your risk tolerance are so important to your 401(k) portfolio.

5. *Select a Diversified Group of Investments:* When I say diversify, that doesn't mean you need one of everything. My "piggy bank" rule is based on the fact that the more money you have on hand to invest, the wider your fund choices can be. Typically, you can build a suitable investment portfolio with as few as four funds, although I recommend more if your company offers a full menu of funds to choose from.

Don't worry if a certain fund class, like emerging-market funds or international funds, doesn't sit well with you. The absence of one fund group isn't going to damage your portfolio. The added comfort you gain by not investing in such a fund is probably worth any moderate gains you might miss out on. With mutual funds, you're already diversified. That's what a mutual fund with investments in 60 or 70 companies can do for you.

Knute's Knotes

Knute's "Piggy Bank" Rule

How much money you have is a big factor in deciding how many mutual funds to invest in. Whether you have $10,000 or $100,000 in your 401(k), here are some guidelines for how many funds you may want to use:

Assets	Maximum Number of Funds
Up to $5,000	1
Up to $50,000	4
Up to $100,000	5
$100K and up	10

One rule says that you should use your age as a barometer in creating an asset allocation plan. It works like this: a 30-year-old train conductor named Ken subtracts his age from 100, giving him 70. That 70 percent represents how much money Ken can invest in stocks; the remainder should be invested in more conservative investments like bonds.

When he turns 40, he bumps his bond holdings up to 40 percent, leaving 60 percent invested in stocks, and so on, until he retires. It's an interesting formula that makes a lot of sense. But as we explain later, it might not be aggressive enough to capitalize on the higher historical stock market returns we've seen over the past 50 years or so.

Whatever asset allocation program you use, try to include a mix of big-company (big-cap) stock funds, small-company (small-cap), and international funds. Then toss into the mix some short- and long-term U.S. Treasury funds and corporate bonds funds. Throw in a money market fund for added protection, and that asset allocation will provide you with the high performers (stocks) and conservative funds (bonds) you need to rest comfortably.

Knute's Knotes

Where Do You Fit in Risk-Wise?

The following tables can help you classify your attitudes as an investor. Do you see anything like your own portfolio here?

Ultra Aggressive Portfolio
35% Small-cap funds
20% International stock funds
20% Sector funds
15% Large-cap funds
10% Emerging-market funds

Aggressive Growth Portfolio
30% International stock funds
35% Large-cap funds
35% Small-cap funds

Growth Portfolio
40% Large-cap funds
25% International stock funds
30% Small-cap funds
5% International bond funds

Growth and Income Portfolio
40% Large-cap growth and income funds
20% Large-cap growth funds
15% International stock funds
15% Small cap funds
10% Intermediate-term bond funds

Conservative Income Portfolio
25% Large-cap growth and income funds
25% Long-term bond funds
20% Intermediate-term bond funds
15% International bond funds
10% International stock funds
5% Small-cap funds

Conservative Portfolio
40% Money-market and short-term bond funds
25% Intermediate-term bond funds
10% International bond funds
10% Large-cap funds
10% International stock funds
5% Small-cap funds

Tips on Choosing Mutual Funds

1. *With mutual funds, size does matter.* When choosing a fund, try to abide by the "$1 billion" rule: if a fund has more than $1 billion in assets, you may want to avoid it. That's because the more money invested in a fund, the harder it can be for a fund manager to sustain the high returns the fund earned when it was smaller and nimbler. Smaller funds have more room to operate and grow.

2. *Age before beauty.* When you're out there kicking tires on mutual funds, trying to decide which one will give you the most mileage, keep this thought in mind: Managers with long track records are usually those with the greatest rate of investment success. Long time managers also foster a sense of stability with their funds. Experience is as important in managing a fund as any other factor I can think of.

3. *Not with my money, you don't.* If the fees and expenses for the fund you're considering are 2 percent or above, you may want to keep looking. High fees drag down the performance of your fund (fund's expenses are tabulated into fund performance). Plus, it's extra money taken out of your pocket that could have been better used elsewhere—like in a lower expense mutual fund.

4. *When it comes to cash, less is more.* If your stock fund is holding more than 10 percent of its assets in cash, that's a sign that the manager thinks the market is heading south fast. The typical cash holdings of domestic stock mutual funds is about 6 percent, with most managers keeping only 2 percent or 3 percent of assets in cash, just to have money on hand to pay for redemptions (i.e., investors who sell their shares in the fund).

   Overall, you don't want to see too much cash on hand. A copy of the semi-annual report or quarterly earnings statements will provide this information. More cash in reserve is less cash working for you in the stock markets.

5. *Look for the proof of the pudding.* Pick stock funds with a track record. That means choosing funds with a performance record of five years or more. There are 6,412 stock funds, compared with 3,105 at the end of 1990, so more than half came into existence in the 1990s, according to the Investment Company Institute in Washington, D.C., the trade association for the fund industry. That, in my opinion, eliminates almost half of the stock funds to choose from.

6. *Change is not always good.* Often, a mutual fund's high turnover rate—the rate of purchases and sales managers made within the fund—can be a red flag for investors. Fund turnover is caused by several factors, including a fund's investment philosophy, changes in market conditions, and even the fund manager's personality. Here's how a fund's turnover rate works: If a fund holds 100 different stocks in its portfolio, and over the course of a year trades 50 of those stocks, then the fund's turnover rate is 50 percent (which is pretty low—the average turnover rate is 90 percent). But a fund with high turnover rates—200 percent or higher—can generate some hefty fees and expenses for shareholders.

High turnover rates of 200 percent or 300 percent not only result in higher expenses, but they can also penalize shareholders through higher capital gains taxes. The more sales and losses realized annually, the more the capital gains tax comes into play.

One caveat: Excessive trading is one thing; opportunistic trading is another. If you notice your fund's turnover rate hovering at about 150 percent, don't worry. At that level, your fund manager may simply be taking advantage of undervalued stocks (particularly in down markets).

Knute's Knotes Worksheet

Test Your Knowledge

Now that you've read up a little bit on mutual funds, studied your risk profile, and learned how to allocate your assets, let's see how much you remember. The following is the *Money Magazine*/Vanguard Mutual Fund Literacy Test: pass it and you've become a graduate of Mutual Fund U. (Answers are on p. 116.)

1. What is the most important benefit you get from creating a diversified portfolio that includes stock, bond, and money market funds?
   A. A guarantee that your portfolio won't suffer if the stock market falls
   B. Higher returns than you get with a portfolio that isn't diversified
   C. The ability to balance both risk and return in achieving your financial goals
   D. All of the above

2. As you approach your investment goal, which one of the following statements is generally most appropriate?
   A. You should be willing to assume more risk with your investments
   B. You should be willing to assume less risk with your investments
   C. You can stop monitoring your investments

3. The process of deciding how your investment dollars will be split among various classes of financial assets such as stocks, bonds, and cash reserves is best described as:

A. Dollar-cost averaging
B. Asset allocation
C. Standard deviation
D. Investing

4. Generally, during retirement, investors should have a portion of their portfolio in stock mutual funds because:
   A. They always provide excellent dividend income
   B. Their returns usually outpace inflation over time
   C. Historical returns show that stocks outperform bonds over the long term
   D. Both B and C

5. Which of the following usually increases the overall risk level in your portfolio?
   A. Shifting your asset mix from bonds to stocks
   B. Shifting your asset mix from stocks to bonds
   C. Shifting your asset mix from stocks to money markets
   D. None of the above

6. Which one of the following types of funds would probably hold the largest proportion of U.S. Treasury bills?
   A. Long-term bond fund
   B. Ginnie Mae fund
   C. Growth and income fund
   D. Money market fund

7. Which type of investment has historically provided the best protection against inflation?
   A. Stocks
   B. Bonds
   C. Cash reserves
   D. None of the above

8. Generally, a portfolio that has 80 percent of its assets invested in growth stocks would be best suited for:
  A. A college fund for a 15-year-old
  B. An individual retirement account for a 35-year-old
  C. An income-producing portfolio for an 86-year-old
  D. None of the above

9. In general, which one of the following types of mutual funds is likely to decline the most when the overall stock market falls?
  A. Aggressive growth fund
  B. Growth and income fund
  C. Bond fund
  D. Money market fund

10. "Emerging market" is the term used to describe each year's best-performing foreign stock market.
  A. True
  B. False

11. If interest rates declined, the price of a bond would:
  A. Increase
  B. Decrease
  C. Stay about the same
  D. It is impossible to predict

12. Compared with the price of a short-term bond, the price of a long-term bond:
  A. Will fluctuate more in response to changes in interest rates
  B. Will fluctuate less in response to changes in interest rates
  C. Will not react at all to changes in interest rates

13. All else being equal, the lower a bond fund's credit quality, the higher its yield.
A. True
B. False

14. If two mutual funds hold the same securities, but one has higher operating expenses than the other, which of the following statements is true?
A. The fund with the higher expenses will have a higher return
B. The fund with the lower expenses will have a higher return
C. You can't say which fund would have a higher return, because expenses have no effect

15. If an investor is in the 31 percent or higher federal tax bracket, which one of the following types of funds usually provides the most after-tax income?
A. Treasury bond funds
B. Money market funds
C. Municipal bond funds

16. Index (or passively managed) funds:
A. Seek to match the investment returns of a specified stock or bond benchmark
B. Try to beat the investment return of a specified stock or bond benchmark
C. Limit themselves to the stocks in the Standard & Poor's 500 Stock Index

17. If I want to change the mix of stocks, bonds, and cash reserves in my portfolio, I can do this by:
A. Changing how I direct my future investments
B. Transferring assets between funds in my portfolio
C. Both of the above
D. None of the above

18. A fund's after-tax return may be influenced by:
   A. The fund's pretax return
   B. Turnover of the fund's holdings
   C. The distribution of capital gains
   D. All of the above

19. In general, for long-term investors, once you select your asset allocation you should stick with it unless your risk tolerance, investing time horizon, or financial situation has changed
   A. True
   B. False

20. A market index is a:
   A. Gauge that measures the potential fluctuation in your stock fund account
   B. Representative group of securities that serves as a barometer for market activity
   C. Stock fund management style that selects stocks based on an analysis of markets and individual companies

Answers:

1. C	6. D	11. A	16. A
2. B	7. A	12. A	17. C
3. B	8. B	13. A	18. D
4. D	9. A	14. B	19. A
5. A	10. B	15. C	20. B

A 401(k) Makeover

Name: Martin D.

Age: 43

Occupation: Air Traffic Controller

Retirement Goal: To retire early and go fishing up in the Great Lakes for the rest of my life. My wife and I both love the outdoors and would love to buy a cabin in the woods.

401(k) Assets: $213,000

Portfolio:
20% Stable value fund
15% Conservative equity income
15% Equity index fund
15% Municipal bond fund
15% International stock fund
20% Growth stock fund

Stocks: Media Logic, Intel, PeopleSoft

Comments: I love my 401(k)! I've learned to max out and contribute to an IRA, where I've got an additional $40,000 stashed away. I don't want to lean too far one way or another, either too aggressive or too conservative. I have taken advantage of expanded options in my 401(k) plan to invest internationally, but that was a pretty risky move for me.

Knute Says

With over $250,000 in your IRA and 401(k), you are well on your way to retire as a 401(k) millionaire with a modest 10 percent average growth rate. You should reach that goal in your early fifties. That will give you plenty of time to fish all of the Great Lakes. You didn't say how your IRA was invested, but your 401(k) portfolio is sound. Keep maxing out your 401(k) and IRA contributions and you'll soon be able to buy the woods—not just the cabin.

7

*You can be young without money
but you can't be old without it.*

—*Tennessee Williams*

The Perils of Procrastination

One of Aesop's classic fables concerns the squirrel who started stocking up early for the long, cold winter ahead and the frivolous squirrel who didn't. When winter came, the second squirrel could only gaze enviously at the pile of acorns the first squirrel had safely tucked away up in his tree. Moral of the story: Start piling up your acorns early.

Yet many younger investors complain that they don't make enough money to participate in a 401(k) plan. I wonder what they'd say if they knew how easy it was to earn over $1 million for retirement by putting away a little over $100 per month.

Take the case of Buddy, a 25-year-old truck driver who makes about $25,000 per year. Buddy says he's got a new convertible to pay off and about $500 in rent a month. But if Buddy stashed away only 6 percent of his salary—about $125 per month—and got a 50 percent company match and a modest 8 percent return from his investments, he could earn $1.1 million by the time he turns 65. And if Buddy socked away 8 percent of his salary (or $167 per month), he'd reap $1.4 million by the time he reached 65. A 10 percent or 12 percent investment return on either sum would earn Buddy about $2 million by retirement. All of this on a $25,000 salary!

Coupled with regular, monthly investments in your 401(k) plan—regardless of what the financial markets are doing—compound interest is your best tool in building a big nest egg for retirement. That's important when you consider that, on average, the cost of consumer goods doubles every 18 years (meaning an $18,000 car today will cost $72,000 in the year 2034). How old will you be then? Will you be able to afford a $72,000 car? You will if you follow my advice. It's not going to be easy to keep ahead of inflation. But we Americans are funny about saving money. Sometimes we assume that someone will come along and save our money for us, or maybe that we'll win the lottery. Either way, we seem to figure, what's the rush to begin saving early?

In a 1998 study by *Money* magazine, 60 percent of Americans said they wanted to retire before age 65. But how many of the survey respondents actually had invested more than $5,000 per year in their 401(k) plan? Only 42 percent. Worse, 41 percent kept their money in low-risk investments like bond or money market mutual funds, thus decreasing their chances of beating inflation by investing in historically higher returning stock funds.

With many Americans waiting until their 30s to start families these days, millions of Americans will find themselves paying their kids' college costs while trying to play catch-up with their 401(k)s, just when their retirement savings plans should be shifting into high gear. Personal issues crop up as well. If you wait until you're 35 or 40 to invest in your 401(k), you'll likely find yourself having to add more cash to your monthly contributions.

You'll also have to invest much more aggressively to gain that extra percentage point or two to make up for lost time. (I prefer an aggressive approach, but not everyone is comfortable with a portfolio full of growth and international stocks.) And if you have plans to retire early, think again. Studies show that the vast majority of successful early retirees began planning for their retirement in their 20s and early 30s. In fact, many baby boomers are resigned to the fact that they'll be working well into their golden years, particularly with the rise in Social Security eligibility to age 66 in 2003 and to age 70 by

2029. According to a 1998 study released by the American Association of Retired Persons, 25 percent of boomers say they'll need to keep working after they turn 65. Add in 4 percent annual inflation and it's easy to see why so many Americans have doubts about meeting their retirement needs.

All that gloom and doom is wearing, but I wouldn't be doing my job if I didn't point out all the obstacles older investors face as compared with younger ones. There are, fortunately, some points in your favor if you are an older worker who hasn't started saving for your retirement

Knute's Knotes

A Boost from Your Budget?

So you say you can't afford to begin saving early? Your salary won't cover it or your bills are too high? Well, maybe buying that pricey new car has slowed you down. When I was beginning to save for retirement, I took a long look at my household budget. Without too much fuss I was able to find hundreds of dollars a month out of our household expenses without depleting our standard of living.

In fact, if you can carve $400 out of your monthly budget—promise yourself you'll just try it—and invest the money instead, in 20 years you'll have amassed $297,830, assuming a 10 percent investment return. Don't forget, that money can continue to grow during the 20 or 30 years you'll likely spend in retirement.

Ways to save: Pay down loans; burn credit cards; buy a used car rather than a new one and keep it running longer; and, of course, take maximum advantage of tax-deferred investments, like IRAs and 401(k)s.

yet: as a seasoned employee, you're going to make significantly more money at age 40 than you did at age 25. Plus, everything is relative. If you waited until age 35 or 40 before starting your 401(k) savings plan, it's much better than waiting until age 50 or not starting at all. Sure, it's going to be a bit harder to save $1 million for retirement if you wait until age 42 to begin saving, but that doesn't mean it can't be done.

When It Comes to 401(k) Investing, Youth Isn't Wasted on the Young

Mick Jagger, who may be a rock-'n'-roller, but isn't much younger than I am, sings a song called "Time Is on My Side." Those lyrics remind me of how fortunate younger investors are in being able to take chances with their early 401(k) investments. In fact, if young workers start investing in their 20s and invest aggressively, their chances of becoming a 401(k) millionaire are sky-high.

Consider this hypothetical scenario. It's the year 2020. Fred is a 65-year-old service technician with a Big Three auto maker. Way back when, around the time Ronald Reagan became president and Bill Gates was just getting his feet wet with Microsoft, 25-year-old Fred began investing $2,000 annually in his 401(k). Over a period of 10 years, that investment earned an annual rate of return of 10 percent. After 10 years, Fred stopped the $2,000 annual contribution to his 401(k). Without adding another dime to it, his original $20,000 investment grew to $672,998, enough perhaps for Fred's long-awaited dream of running his own pub in Ireland.

Now let's consider Bob, a 65-year-old computer salesman who waited until age 35 to invest in his 401(k). Even though Bob invested the same $2,000 that Fred did every year and earned the same 10 percent return, Bob needed 30 years to save $400,275, or about $272,000 less than Fred had saved in only 10 years. Amazingly, the early investor—even though he stopped investing after 10 years—saved a lot more money than the investor who started later and had to save for 30 years.

Investing early not only gives you more cash for retirement, it's also a big money-saver: the sooner you start, the less it costs to reach your retirement goals.

Say you want to save $250,000 for retirement. That's low in my book, but let's just use that number as a hypothetical example. Over a 30-year period, you'd need to invest $168 per month at an 8 percent annual interest to reach that goal. But over a shorter time span, things go a little haywire. Over 20 years, you'd need to save $424 per month at the same rate of return to reach your financial goal. And over 10 years, you'd need to save $1,367 per month at the same rate of return! And woe to the worker who waits until he has just 5 years left until retirement. That poor soul would need to save an eye-popping $3,402 per month to keep up with the others.

Things usually get better financially as you get older. You earn more money, maybe you've paid off your mortgage, maybe the kids have moved out. But $3,402 per month? You'd have to be in pretty unusual circumstances to be able to pull that off.

To reach a savings goal of $250,000 at age 55, you'd need to save the following amounts monthly, based on your age (and an 8 percent annual return):

Age	Amount Saved per Month
25	$ 168
35	424
45	1,367
50	3,402

Procrastination is always a bad idea, but it *is* relative. In the previous example, we cited Fred, who started saving at age 25 and stopped 10 years later. The numbers show that Fred kicked the 35-year-old Bob's tail in terms of their 401(k) savings' ability. But compared to 46-year-old Beth, who just started saving, Bob's situation looks a tad rosier. The earlier compounding begins, the higher your money grows. (Chart assumes 10 percent average annual return based on S&P 500 performance from December 31, 1925, to December 31, 1996 [10.78%].)

THE PERILS OF PROCRASTINATION II

Age	Bob's Cumulative Investment	Total Value at 10 Percent Annual Return	Beth's Cumulative Investment	Total Value at 10 Percent Annual Return
36	$ 3,000	$ 3,168		
37	6,000	6,667		
38	9,000	10,533		
39	12,000	14,803		
40	15,000	19,521		
41	18,000	24,732		
42	21,000	30,490		
43	24,000	36,850		
44	27,000	43,876		
45	30,000	51,638		
46		57,045	$ 3,000	$ 3,168
47		63,018	6,000	6,667
48		69,617	9,000	10,533
49		76,907	12,000	14,803
50		84,960	15,000	19,521
51		93,856	18,000	24,732
52		103,685	21,000	30,490
53		114,542	24,000	36,850
54		126,536	27,000	43,876
55		139,786	30,000	51,638
56		154,424	33,000	60,212
57		170,594	36,000	69,685
58		188,457	39,000	80,149
59		208,191	42,000	91,710
60		229,992	45,000	104,481
61		254,075	48,000	118,589
62		280,680	51,000	134,174
63		310,070	54,000	151,392
64		342,539	57,000	170,412
65		378,407	60,000	191,424
Total	$30,000	$378,407	$60,000	$191,424

So, although Bob got off to a bit of a late start, especially when compared to 25-year-old Fred, he handily outpaced Beth, who waited until age 46 to begin contributing to her 401(k) plan. In fact, Beth contributed twice as much money—$60,000 versus $30,000—and still fell short of Bob's retirement earnings by about $175,000.

More to the point, Beth is going to have to double up on her monthly contributions to catch up to younger longer term savers like Bob or Fred. That's what I mean when I say starting early actually helps you *save* money. So write out this slogan and tack it to your bulletin board at work, your bathroom mirror at home, or anywhere you can't fail to be influenced by it every day:

A LITTLE MONEY EARLY GOES A LONG WAY LATER.

Knute's Knotes

A Way to Gauge How Fast Your 401(k) Investments Double

Looking for a way to measure how fast your money grows in your 401(k)? Look no further. The Rule of 72 enables you to calculate how long it will take your money to double at a given rate of return (providing you reinvest your earnings—and if you're reading this book, you better be).

Here's a brief primer: Simply divide the number 72 by the annual percentage rate you are receiving on that sum of money. For example, at a rate of 8 percent, an investment's value will double in 9 years (72 divided by 8 = 9). At 10 percent, it would take 7.2 years for your money to double (72 divided by 10 = 7.2). The Rule of 72 also works for calculating the costs of inflation. At 4 percent inflation, the price of a gallon of milk will double in 18 years.

Check out the following table to see clearly how the Rule of 72 works:

Rate of Return	Years to Double	Rate of Return	Years to Double
1%	72	11%	6.5
2	36	12	6.0
3	24	13	5.5
4	18	14	5.1
5	14.4	15	4.8
6	12	16	4.5
7	10.3	17	4.2
8	9	18	4.0
9	8	19	3.8
10	7.2	20	3.6

Note that the higher rates of return double your money in a shorter time span.

Knute's Knotes

You Can Never Start Early Enough

The beauty of starting an early investment program is that age doesn't matter—a parent could start an investment account chock full of high-performing mutual funds for her newborn baby.

In fact, many Americans saving for their children's future—whether that includes a college education or simply help in getting a leg up on life—prefer to open up custodial accounts, like the Uniform Gift to Minors Act (UGMA) or Uniform Transfer to Minors Act (UTMA). These accounts take a cash gift from a parent, grandparent, or family friend acting as custodian (or caretaker) and invest it in mutual funds. Most mutual fund companies offer them, too. When your child turns 18, the money is waiting to be collected. Custodial accounts are a tax benefit to you as well. They enable you to shift income from you, in your higher tax bracket, to your children, in their lower tax bracket.

Custodial accounts are relatively easy to open and you can contribute any amount you like. Even a few dollars a month can add up if you begin when your kids are toddlers. Under current Internal Revenue Service statutes, the first $700 of net income and gains from your investment for a child under age 14 is tax-free and the next $700 is taxed at the child's rate, likely 15 percent. Above the $1,400 level, income and gains are taxed at the parent's marginal rate until the child turns 14. After that, all income and gains are taxed at the child's rate.

The lone downside to UGMAs and UTMAs is that once the money is placed into the account, the IRS considers it an irrevocable gift. That means that when the cash is distributed when your son or daughter turns 18, your child can use the money any way he or she wants. You may have worked hard to save for college funds or to get your children off to a good independent start, but you will have nothing to say if they decide to give all the money to charity or to a cult. Many parents prefer to leave the money in a mutual fund account or begin rolling it over into an IRA every year.

It's not too hard to show your kids how fast the money grows and how much they're accumulating at an early age. Just show them the charts and tables in this chapter. The lesson you teach by instilling your progeny with a sense of financial discipline will be invaluable to them. Don't ever think you have to wait until you bring home a big, fat paycheck to start saving for your golden years. By investing early, even a young paralegal just starting out or a fresh-out-of high school assembly line worker with an entry-level salary can easily save $1 million for retirement.

I have five children. When they each reached high school age, I told them that if they didn't start smoking, I would put away the cost of one pack of cigarettes a day (about $900 a year) for one year into a mutual fund with their name on it. I put the money into an index fund and by the time each of my children is 65 years old, the fund should be worth almost a quarter of a million dollars. And, they don't smoke, either. They have learned two lessons.

The most important thing to remember about starting early is that nobody—not your mother, father, boss, spouse, or lover is going to hand you a $1 million check when you retire. You've got to take care of it yourself. And you don't have a minute to lose.

Knute's Knotes

The Folly of Too Much Company Stock

Owning company stock in your 401(k) plan is great if you work for Microsoft or Coca-Cola. But too much stock in most companies can cause heartburn for the healthiest 401(k) plan. Unfortunately, that's something your employer doesn't want you to know. According to a 1998 study by Hewitt Associates, employer stocks average 33 percent of 401(k) assets at companies that include company stocks as a 401(k) investment option. More than half of the 450 mid- to large-sized companies participating in the study offer company stock in their 401(k) plans, up from 36 percent in 1996.

With over 20 percent or 30 percent of your portfolio reserved for your employer's stock, a slide in the company's fortunes can spell big trouble for your retirement. Big losses could translate into a double-digit drop in your 401(k), even if the rest of the economy is doing great. And, if you're a big investor in company stock and the company suffers big losses in any given year, you face the potentially horrifying prospect of losing your bonus, your job, plus a big chunk of your retirement earnings.

Not only does too much employer stock give your 401(k) plan an imbalanced look, but it doesn't perform as well as regular stocks. For the 12-month period from September 30, 1996, to September 30, 1997, company stocks (at 34.6%) lagged behind the S&P 500 Index (at 40.6%).

Remember the plight of IBM workers in the late 1980s? In 1987, Big Blue's stock was trading at $175 a share. Misfortune ensued and the company's stock slid over the next six years, bottoming out at $2 in 1993. Not coincidentally, IBM began instituting big layoffs during the same time, even though the stock eventually started climbing again.

If you like your company stock and you want to include it in your 401(k), keep the asset allotment below 10 percent. Use the rest of the money to invest in other aggressive stock funds, like small-company or international stock funds. Stock funds are safer than individual stocks because they include a wide variety of stocks. Remember, it's up to you—not your employer—to come up with the cash you need for retirement. Nobody's going to bail you out if things go bad at the plant or office. Keep that in mind the next time your boss urges you to push more company stock into your 401(k).

A 401(k) Makeover

Name: Dan R.

Age: 28

Occupation: Golf instructor

Retirement Goals: I want my wife and I to save enough money to buy a second home in Naples, Florida, and spend our winters down there. I could teach golf on the side and maybe even take a run at the Senior PGA tour.

401(k) Assets: $47,200

Portfolio: 40% Small-cap growth stocks
20% Mid-cap growth stocks
10% Large company stock fund
30% Foreign company stocks

Stocks: Carver, Inc., Warner Lambert, Dell Computer

Comments: I like to take chances and I believe in doing that with my retirement funds. My wife doesn't approve and her 401(k) is much more conservative. I figure since I'm young I have a lot of time until retirement so if the stock market tanks, I'll have time to make it all up.

Knute Says

Your philosophy is on target. With 30 years to go before retirement, you will have the time to make up any market downturns. In fact, since 1929 there is no five-year period where the S&P 500 has lost money. I'm not a big fan, however, of individual stocks in a retirement portfolio. When your portfolio gets large, you would need too many stocks to be adequately diversified and to keep track of that many separate companies may prove too much to handle. I suggest that you keep the same percentages as you have but instead of 30 percent in foreign company stocks, put that 30 percent into an international mutual fund with a good long-term track record. Pay that professional money manager his 1 percent fee—it's well worth it. The same thing applies to your small and mid-cap stocks.

8

*Without discipline, there's no life
at all.*

—Katharine Hepburn

Maxing Out: More
Money for You—and
Less for Uncle Sam

There's no getting around it. Each month brings with it a new set of bills: mortgage, car insurance, utilities, phone—and retirement. That's right, retirement. When you treat your 401(k) plan like any other household expense, you will be sure to keep "paying it off" every month. And the more tax-deferred money you pay yourself, the more you keep for yourself—and away from Uncle Sam.

Unfortunately not every American is getting the picture. According to Access Research, Inc., by not fully investing in their 401(k)s, employees are ignoring $6 billion in free 401(k) money. For the life of me I can't figure that one out. If you found a $100 bill on the sidewalk, you'd pick it up, wouldn't you? So would I! But many investors aren't taking advantage of free goodies like employee matching and maximum contribution limits.

I'm concerned about this country's lax savings habits. Congress is worried, too. Right now, the median income of retirees is only $11,533. Almost two-thirds of American workers are saving little or nothing for retirement, and the outlook, if nothing changes, is grim. Congressional proposals like a hike in the 401(k) distribution cap from 1998's $10,000 limit to $15,000, and a higher cap on total contributions (including employer contributions) to a flat ceiling of $45,000 (or 25 percent of pay) are currently being debated in Washington. Another proposal would allow fiftysomethings to raise their 401(k) investment ceiling from $10,000 to $20,000. (Wow! Imagine if you'd been saving all along and then, bam, you've got an extra $10,000 tax-deferred investment cap when you turn 50?)

But you know how slowly the wheels grind in Washington. For now, it's up to you to maximize your contribution and take full advantage of fat employee-matching programs. At the same time, investing regularly remains as important as ever. I've always maintained that one of the best deals associated with your 401(k) plan is that your employer will deduct monthly contributions from your paycheck automatically and plug them into your 401(k) plan. It's convenient and painless. You don't have to do anything!

While automatic deductions can't guarantee a profit or protect against a loss, they do prevent you from doing a horrible thing with your money: nothing. (See the section on dollar-cost averaging later in this chapter for more information on saving money through regular monthly contributions to your 401(k)).

Knute's Knotes

Company Matching Information That Your Boss May Not Want You to Know

Company matching is the pot of gold at the end of the rainbow. A common scenario is that your boss matches 50 cents to every dollar you put in to your 401(k), up to a limit. So if you make $50,000 annually and contribute 6 percent of your salary ($3,000) to your 401(k), you will receive $1,500 gratis from your employer. Free money! And it's better than a raise because it's tax-deferred.

But not all company match policies are created equal. There are some strings attached to certain employee matching plans that you should know about. For example, some companies make their company stock part of the deal. As I've mentioned, having too much company stock in your 401(k) is a bad idea. It's usually in your employer's best interest, not yours.

Some companies also make the employee-matching deal contingent on your sticking around a while. If you plan on leaving after three years, for example, you could lose money promised you by the company (that's called "vesting"). In many cases, companies are betting that you won't last the five years needed to be completely vested and qualify for your employee matching benefits. Some companies are even so brazen as to take the employee-matched earnings your 401(k) made up to that point and keep it themselves if you leave your position before you're vested. So if your stock fund gained 35 percent one year and your employer matched 50 percent of your contributions, but you left shortly afterward, your employer will help themselves to one-third of your profits.

The same companies will turn around and use that money as employee matching for the 401(k) plan of the person who replaces you. If he or she doesn't stay, they'll take a chunk of those 401(k) earnings, and so on and so on. It's no wonder companies are so generous with their 401(k) employee matching programs! After a modest initial investment, some never pay so much as a dime into them!

Big (and Steady) Contributions Win the Race

Think about it. Early-bird investors who contribute anywhere from $50 to $500 every month for 30 or 40 years are going to be mighty comfortable in retirement. At age 25 or 30, the numbers are heavily in your favor.

It's even better when you save regularly and save a lot. The more you save each month, the more money you'll have in retirement. Consider the experiences of four different investors, all of whom started contributing to their 401(k) plan at age 25, but who contributed different amounts.

- Lynn understood the benefits of starting early, but could only afford to sock away $50 into her 401(k) plan.
- Corrado was an early-bird, too, and was eager to put a little more money aside for retirement. He saved $100 monthly.
- Molly was even more aggressive, staking $200 of her pay each month toward her 401(k).
- Karl was positively giddy about being a 401(k) millionaire, putting away a whopping $500 per month toward his golden years.

Knute's Knotes

When's a Good Time to Start?

I run into a lot of people who ask me when is the best time to get into the stock market. I say anytime is a good time and now is the best time.

Consider a worst case scenario. If you had invested $2,000 in the stock market every year for the past 25 years, buying at the top of the market where prices are highest, you still would have made over five times your original investment. A total investment of $50,000 would be worth $281,000 today. But if you'd played it safe and remained in Treasury bills, you'd only have made half as much. And if you invested nothing, well. . . .

Here's how they made out (based on a hypothetical, 10 percent average annual rate of return) over a 25-year period:

Age 25	Monthly Saving	Age 50
Lynn	$ 50	$ 66,895
Corrado	100	133,789
Molly	200	267,568
Karl	500	668,945

As you can see, Karl and Molly are well on their way to becoming 401(k) millionaires by the time they retire at age 65. Lynn and Corrado should make it, but beefing up their monthly investing contributions would provide a big boost to their retirement fund.

A steady investment stream every month into your 401(k) is more than worth the trouble. But if you want to make a real difference in your financial future, invest a big chunk of money every month.

Dollar-Cost Averaging: More Investments for Your Money

I always recommend the regular investment approach. It gets you into the habit of investing and it's the best way to grow retirement assets. But everyone has a favorite way of investing money. There's no shortage of strategies to get you saving regularly to maximum effect. Each comes with its own set of rules and regulations, except for one ironclad rule: The market is volatile. The value of stocks and bonds will *always* fluctuate.

A great way to take advantage of that volatility, invest regularly, and make some money in the bargain is through dollar-cost averaging—the technique of investing equal dollar amounts on a fixed schedule, no matter what the market is doing. When you participate in dollar-cost averaging, you buy more shares when prices are low and fewer shares when prices are high. It protects against investing too large an amount at a market peak. Dollar-cost averaging is most suitable for the long-term investor who seeks to accumulate wealth by religiously plowing money into the market.

While you can use dollar-cost averaging with individual stocks, it's more commonly used by funds investors, who don't trade funds as often as stock investors trade stocks. While dollar-cost averaging won't significantly increase your investment returns, it will add discipline to your investing habits by forcing you to invest regularly. The following chart reveals that dollar-cost averaging enables you to buy more mutual fund shares when prices are low and fewer when prices are high, thereby giving you the most bang for your investment buck.

DOLLAR-COST AVERAGING VARIATIONS IN RISING, DECLINING, AND FLUCTUATING MARKETS

Regular Investment	Rising Market		Declining Market		Fluctuating Market	
	Share Price	Shares Acquired	Share Price	Shares Acquired	Share Price	Shares Acquired
$ 400	$ 5	80	$16	25	$10	40
400	8	50	10	40	8	50
400	10	40	8	50	5	80
400	10	40	8	50	8	50
400	16	25	5	80	10	40
$2,000	$49	235	$47	245	$41	260

Average share cost:

$8.51	$8.16	$7.69
($2,000/235)	($2,000/245)	($2,000 /260)

Average share price:

$9.80	$9.40	$8.20
($49/5)	($47/5)	($41/5)

In the 401(k) package your mutual fund provider gives you when you enroll in your company's plan, there's bound to be a healthy section or two on dollar-cost averaging. The technique is manna from heaven for fund companies because it provides a steady revenue stream for them. Ask any fund marketer and she'll tell you that inflows are much better than outflows for mutual fund companies.

But one paragraph in the dollar-cost averaging section of your 401(k) kit calls for closer examination. It's the one that tells you that dollar-cost averaging offers no assurance that you'll make a profit or be protected against a loss in declining markets. While dollar-cost averaging is a useful investment strategy, it's not a *guarantee*.

That said, the thing I like best about dollar-cost averaging, even better than the lower share costs derived from it, is the fact that it disciplines you to invest in your 401(k) every month, no matter what the financial markets are doing.

(Market) Timing Isn't Everything

Although I like pounding home the benefits of investing regularly, I don't like participating in market timing strategies. Market timers say it's perfectly normal and totally possible to move all your investment assets around in order to take advantage of market upticks and to minimize losses during market declines. In other words, market-timers think they can guess when the time is right to buy or sell securities.

That sounds great, right? Who wouldn't want to know when the stock market is going up and when it's going down? The trouble with market-timers is that they *don't* know. Or if they do, they don't have the time to update their charts and spreadsheets to take advantage of it. As I mentioned before, I'm a reformed market-timer who found it energy-depleting to try to go to work, provide for my family, be a good husband and father, and, oh yeah, track IBM's earnings cycles every night.

Plus, market-timing strategy is dubious at best. It's like driving in the middle lane on the expressway. The left lane is flying by, so you switch over to gain speed. Suddenly, it's the right lane that's moving swiftly, so you switch lanes again. Then the middle lane looks smoother, so you hop over again. That's what market timing is like: trying to guess which lane moves fastest. Ultimately, you're going to spend as much time weaving in and out of traffic as you are moving forward.

Market timers compound their own problems by being out of the market when they shouldn't be. Looking to catch a perceived market wave, these market surfers buy days (even hours) after a sustained market rally or sell just after a big market meltdown, like the ones we saw in October 1987, October 1997, and September 1998. All that moving around means that market-timers actually miss the best times to be in the stock market.

A market-timing study done by the University of Michigan bears this out. From December 31, 1981, to August 25, 1987, stocks returned on average 26.3 percent annually. But to market timers who were busy during that period hopping in and out of the market like an over egg-nogged Peter Rabbit, and happened to miss the best 10 days over that 6-year time span when the markets took off, the price was heavy. Instead of earning the 26 percent the buy-and-holders received, the market timers only earned 18.3 percent. That's about two-thirds of the stock market's average return over that time—and I'm not even counting the additional hundreds and thousands of dollars spent on trading commissions and taxes incurred from frequent trading.

Missing the best 10 days of a bull market is one thing. Imagine missing the best 40 days of the 1980's bull market. Note the comparison between the buy-and-hold investor who remained in the stock market during the entire period from December 21, 1981, through August 25, 1987, and the market-timer who missed the top 40 days of market performance.

THE COST OF BEING "OUT OF THE MARKET" 1982–1987 (PERIOD ENDING AUGUST 25, 1987)

Investment Period	Average Annual Return (%)	Percent of Return Missed
Entire 1,276 trading days	+26.3	0.0
Less the 10 biggest days	+18.3	30.4
Less the 20 biggest days	+13.1	50.2
Less the 30 biggest days	+8.5	67.7
Less the 40 biggest days	+4.3	83.7

Source: University of Michigan.

Make Investing a Habit

I know what you're thinking: it's easy for high-salaried executives to contribute regularly—after all, they're making the big bucks. It's tougher for the rest of us working stiffs.

Yes, that's true. A study done by the accounting firm of KPMG Peat Marwick showed that 90 percent of white-collar workers participated in their company 401(k) plans, compared to 64 percent of blue-collar workers. But once they figure out how easy and rewarding it is to build up $1 million in their 401(k)s, I can't believe the blue-collar workers won't jump in smiling.

Knute's Knotes

The 401(k) vs. Traditional Mutual Funds

Regular investing in a 401(k) plan shouldn't be confused with regular contributions to a mutual fund (although the latter is a great idea if you've maxed out on your 401(k) and IRA plans).

A 401(k) plan's tax-advantaged status outweighs any benefits you get from your regular mutual fund portfolio. Your 401(k) plan investments are not taxed until you retire (presumably when you're in a much lower tax bracket). Better yet, your payroll deductions decrease your taxable income, thus reducing your income tax bill come April 15.

A 401(k) Makeover

Name: Peggy K.

Age: 50

Occupation: Security guard

Retirement Goals: To retire at age 55, with Social Security, my company pension, and 401(k) as my primary means of support during retirement. My kids are out on their own and my husband and I would like to take the snowbird route down south to either New Mexico or Arizona and play tennis and golf and live the good life.

401(k) Assets: $567,000

Portfolio: 25% Company stock
25% Equity income fund
25% Growth fund
25% High-grade corporate bond fund

Stocks: None

Comments: I've always been very good about maxing out on my 401(k) since I got it into it 16 years ago. I usually contribute 15% of my salary and I think that's really paid off. I'm tempted to be more driven with stocks, but I always shy away at the last minute. I don't want to roll the dice and lose everything. On the other hand, I'd love as much money as I could get from my 401(k) in retirement.

Knute Says

At first glance, your retirement portfolio looks just about right—a conservative portfolio, a company pension plan and Social Security. But is it really right? With 25 percent of your portfolio in company stock *and* a company pension plan, you have put too many eggs in one basket! Cash out all of your company stock into an index fund. If anything unfortunate happens at your company, you may be out of a job, out of a pension, and have a big loss in your 401(k) portfolio. Otherwise your portfolio and your attitude look great.

9

*We can add to our knowledge, but
we cannot at will subtract from it.*
—*Arthur Koestler*

Learning the Ropes:
Your Inner Savvy Investor

Your march to your 401(k) million will be much smoother if you stop regularly to learn more about how Wall Street works. Just breezing daily through *The Wall Street Journal,* or monthly through some sound investment newsletters or magazines can beef up your investment know-how. Not surprisingly, that knowledge enhances your chances of becoming a 401(k) millionaire.

The advantages of boning up on mutual funds and investment management are obvious: Experience shows that experience counts. 401(k) participants who prepare and plan for retirement—which includes knowing as much as possible about investing—fare better than those who leave their financial futures to chance and who can't be bothered to read the business section of the newspaper or attend an investment seminar.

That's what my third rule of 401(k) success is all about—how to make you the master of your financial domain through self-education. In this chapter, we'll examine some investment books, magazines, and newsletters, explain how to make sense of stock, mutual fund tables, and investment prospectuses, and learn the value of investment seminars and investment clubs. You've already learned the hard stuff: how the financial markets work, determining risk and reward, and how to allocate your assets.

Knute's Knotes

Fueling Investment Knowledge at Mobil Oil

Mobil Oil offers their lucky employees not one, not two, but three financial management classes. There's a basic money management class, which is an all-day seminar that covers budgeting and other money fundamentals; a two-hour investment class that covers the ins and outs of the financial markets; and a preretirement two-day workshop for employees nearing retirement.

Mobil also offers employees telephone hotlines, one-on-one financial counseling, and interactive money management software tools. Mobil says that financially secure workers are happy workers. Its employees say that it's a relief to have somewhere to go for advice on their 401(k) plans. Both employer and employee have reason to smile.

According to a 1997 study by Virginia Tech Economics Professor Tom Garman, 45 percent of workers have money troubles and a third of those have what Garman considers "serious" money woes. But the study concludes that employer-sponsored financial training can alleviate some of those money problems through a little education while saving companies $400 per year in lost productivity and absenteeism that Garman traces back to employee's money problems.

That's the kind of win-win situation I like.

According to a recent survey conducted by KPMG Peat Marwick, employee financial education training, like seminars and classes, increases 401(k) participation more than any other factor, including

146

employee matching. Even more relevant to you, investment education also increases the amount of money participants contribute to their 401(k)s. And that, my friends, is the name of the game: putting more money into your financial future.

The study also notes that the biggest beneficiaries of employer-sponsored financial training are lower paid workers. With a little prodding, anyone, no matter how small a paycheck, can actively increase his or her investment knowledge while socking away more money in a 401(k) plan. The median account balance is $8,250 at companies that provide some sort of investment training, but only $5,000 at companies that don't.

Unfortunately, many companies shy away from offering direct financial help to employees, fearing that help might be misconstrued as financial advice. In our litigation-happy society, companies can be held liable for investment losses if employees claim they acted on an employer's advice. Unless you work for a company that downplays that risk and offers financial training anyway (and a few, such as Mobil Oil, Oracle, and Fujitsu America, are doing just that), the bulk of your financial education will be up to you.

Questions to Ask at
Employer-Sponsored Financial Seminars

If there's only one thing you should know about investment seminars, it's this: don't ever pay to attend one. Fly-by-night hucksters make a financial killing on naive investors who fork over hundreds of dollars to hear half-baked ideas on investing and listen to promises of 300 percent annualized returns in one year. Trust me, they don't work. Paid seminars are fools' gold. The only guaranteed way of making money on Wall Street is by doing your homework and honing the investment basics.

Free seminars, on the other hand, such as those offered by most financial advisors, brokerage houses, and fund companies, offer good value, if you can ignore the inevitable sales pitch. They don't charge

147

anything and the coffee is good and hot. If you're employer offers you a chance to attend a financial seminar, jump on it!

Employee-sponsored investment seminars are a great opportunity to learn more about your company's 401(k) plan and see how it's doing. Typically, a company offering such a seminar will bring in a financial planner or a representative from the fund company managing your 401(k) money. When Q & A time arrives, don't be shy. Ask as many questions as you can—you'll learn more and maybe wind up investing more in your 401(k).

Here are some key issues to cover with your seminar experts:

1. *Ask about fees.* If you don't get the straight skinny on your plan's 401(k) fees, you might be losing money you never knew you had. Ask how much your plan fees are, what services you get for those fees, and whether the fees are apt to change anytime soon. Also, ask what the plan's annual investment expenses are. Then ask how those expenses compare to your fund's expenses. They should only amount to about 1 percent of your plan assets. A good instructor will demonstrate how yearly fees and expenses can impact performance over a 10-, 20-, or 30-year period.

2. *Check out performance.* If your seminar presenter is a representative from the fund company, and he or she doesn't bring up the issue of plan performance, bring it up yourself. Ask what funds in your 401(k) plan are performing best and why. And check out the benchmarks that your funds' performance are compared against. For example, a typical growth stock fund is usually compared to the Standard & Poor's 500 Index. If your growth fund is returning 10 percent while the S&P 500 is averaging 15 percent over the past year, you deserve to know why.

3. *Ask about plan options.* If there are only three or four options, why not more? Is there an international or global fund in your plan? If not, why not? Is your plan heavy with bond funds or other conservative funds? If so, ask why.

Investment Table Talk

To novice investors, the language used in newspaper stock and mutual fund tables might as well be written in ancient Greek. As a result, many Americans participating in 401(k) plans don't crack open the paper every morning and check on the performance of their plan's mutual funds.

Understanding investment tables is really quite simple. Whether you're reading *The Wall Street Journal* or *The Podunk Gazette*, stock tables are usually the same. The goal of investment tables is to summarize the daily trading activity in individual stocks, bonds, and mutual funds. Most newspapers concentrate on the New York Stock Exchange or the American Stock Exchange and leave the regional exchanges out.

Mutual funds are handled a bit differently. The major funds are included in the daily newspaper listings, but with over 6,500 funds out there, no newspaper has the size to include the performance of each one. But most of the funds included in 401(k) plans are of ample size and stature to be included in abbreviated listings.

There are four key pieces of information in a stock table. The company's name is usually the first item you'll see. Often, longer company names like Home Depot or Microsoft are abbreviated (HomDep, Msoft) to fit into the newspaper's limited space. Some papers use the company's stock trading symbol, characterized by two, three, or four upper-case letters that closely resemble the company's name. For example, General Motor's stock symbol is GM. Next you see the term div for dividend, then close for the closing price of the stock on the previous trading day. Last, you'll see Chg for change, meaning the percentage the stock went up or down depending on the previous day's trading activity.

Let's use GM as an example and create an actual line in *The Philadelphia Inquirer*'s stock trading table:

Name	Div.	Close	Chg.
GM	2.00	71⅜₆	−2

In the first column, General Motor's name is abbreviated. The second column shows the company's annual per share dividend (usually noted in dollars and cents and based on the company's last distribution). In GM's case that's $2.00 per share. The third column represents the previous day's closing trading price for GM ($71³/₁₆). And column four shows how much money the stock gained or lost, in this case a decline of $2.00 from the previous day's trading.

Often newspapers will toss in 52-week highs and lows, which is exactly what it sounds like: the company's highest trading price and lowest trading price over the past year. I find 52-week highs and lows helpful, because they provide a benchmark of how successful or how poorly the stock performed over a year's time.

Mutual fund stock tables are even easier to understand. Individual funds are usually grouped under the name of the company that offers them. For example, American Century's listing includes all of its funds, alphabetized from the company's Gift Trust fund to its Vista fund:

Name	NAV	Chg	12-Mo. Rtn. %
American Century			
Vista Fund	12.81	+.02	−1.90

The table includes the company and fund name (the fund company is listed only once, at the top of the group listing). NAV stands for the net asset value of each fund share in dollars and cents. Usually, the NAV does not reflect the previous day's redemptions (sales of the fund by shareholders). Chg is exactly the same as in the stock table, the rate at which the fund's NAV rose or fell the previous day. Twelve-mo. Rtn. % is the percentage that the fund increased or decreased over the past year. In Vista's case, the fund has lost 1.90 percent of its worth from the same date the previous year.

Most newspapers include a "how to read the stock and mutual fund tables" box on the financial page, usually below the first stock and mutual fund listings. They include sample lines and glossaries of symbols and terms used.

It doesn't have to be difficult to follow your money. The news you need is right under your nose every day, in your morning paper. So go ahead and check on your favorite stock or mutual fund every morning. Pretty soon, if you're like me, you'll make a game of it and compare the performance of your funds with others in its group. Before you know it, you'll be a genuine market guru.

Understanding a Mutual Fund Prospectus

Unlike easy-to-read stock tables, making sense of mutual fund prospectuses can be as painful as a root canal. The legal and financial terminology used in prospectuses make reading one an experience only a masochist or government bureaucrat could love.

Much to the dismay of lawyers everywhere (who earn big bucks by writing and interpreting the cumbersome documents), mutual fund prospectuses have undergone a big facelift recently. The Securities and Exchange Commission (SEC) has forced fund companies to simplify the language of their prospectuses. The result? Plain English mutual fund prospectuses that are easier to read and understand, and offer more protection for investors who might have missed a crucial bit of fund information in the confusing prospectuses of old. By law, fund companies are to switch to plain English prospectuses by January 1, 1999.

When it comes to mutual fund prospectuses, the government is in your corner. Under the new SEC rules, fund companies must adhere to six basic writing principles geared to easier readability: no passive voice, shorter sentences, everyday words, lists of bulleted points for complex materials, no legal jargon or highly technical business terms, and no multiple negatives. In short, Uncle Sam is shooting for a more conversational prospectus, one that all of us can understand.

Before the SEC stepped in, user-friendliness took a back seat to jargon and bloated sentences like the following one: "The applicability of the general information and administrative procedures set forth below accordingly will vary depending on the investor and the record-keeping system established for a shareholder's investment in the fund." Is it any wonder that most fund prospectuses go right from the mailbox into the recycling bin?

Business Week magazine recently published a revealing before/after comparison of mutual prospectus jargon. Compare the old version of an actual fund company prospectus with the new one:

Old version: "The fund utilizes a strategy of investing in those common stocks which have records of having increased their shareholder dividend in each of the preceding ten years or more."

New version: "The fund's stock investments are exclusively in companies that have increased their dividend payout in each of the last ten years."

Old version: "The net asset value of the fund's shares fluctuates as market conditions change."

New version: "The fund's shares will rise and fall in value."

Now if only the SEC could step in and simplify assembly instructions for appliances and toys, my life would be complete.

In defense of the fund companies, they are under constant pressure to satisfy the fiduciary demands of Uncle Sam. That's why every potential fund shareholder receives a prospectus and an application form before buying shares in a fund. The idea is that you'll read the prospectus and know what you're investing in before you complete the application and cut the fund company a check for your shares.

It's in your best interests to know what's in the prospectus, simplified or not. Here are key questions your prospectus should answer:

1. *The fund's investment objective.* Is your fund taking an aggressive, moderate, or conservative approach? The prospectus will tell you.
2. *What's the risk?* Is your fund playing around with riskier investments like options, currencies, and other derivatives? Is it investing overseas when it's not supposed to be? Earlier prospectuses were notoriously lax in describing a fund's risk parameters. Most prospectuses would issue a laundry list of "possible" investments and assign risk categories to each one. Under the new SEC rules, fund companies must list what percent a fund is investing in international funds, instead of issuing bland statements that there is a "possibility" at any given time the fund has gone fishing in overseas waters.

3. *Investment performance.* Mutual funds must list in the prospectus returns for the past 10 years. You'll find the fund's performance history for 1 year, 3 years, 5 years, and 10 years (if the fund has been around that long). Those numbers will paint a picture of how the fund has performed in good and bad markets. Check out the fund's portfolio manager: Has he or she been with the fund a while or just a year or so? Typically, funds do better with the same hands on the steering wheel for a few years.

4. *Tax consequences.* Most mutual funds require that you pay taxes on all dividends and capital gains earned when holding the fund. But some funds handle these distributions differently and thus offer different scenarios for your potential tax consequences.

5. *A listing of all fund fees.* This is where older prospectuses threw a lot of numbers and symbols at shareholders. With the new simplified prospectuses, fund companies have to list their fund fees in a straightforward fashion, summarizing (in a user-friendly format) 12b-1 fees, sales charges, and any other fees associated with the fund.

Going Clubbing

Groucho Marx said he wouldn't join any club that would have him as a member. I bet he never tried to join an investment club. I like investment clubs. I know, some of them get a bad rap from professional money managers who liken them to amateur hour at the local comedy club. I've seen studies that indicate investment clubs do better or as well as professional investors, and I've seen studies that say investment clubs fare poorly when compared to Wall Street's best.

None of that matters to me. I'm an advocate of investing by any means possible. If joining an investment club means that you'll get more serious about your finances and more knowledgeable about the stock market, then I say go for it!

This is especially true for beginners. Investment clubs can be a great source of new investment ideas and strategies and an interesting forum for truly democratic investing: the best stock-picking ideas are pushed to the forefront by group consensus.

Investment clubs are hardly new, although they've grown by leaps and bounds in the past 20 years. According to the National Association of Investor Corporation, which offers educational materials and how-to kits to prospective investment clubbers, member clubs operating under its banner have burgeoned to 37,000 clubs from 3,642 in 1980.

The fastest-growing segment of investment club participants is composed of groups that are traditionally underrepresented in investment circles. Women, for example, have seen their numbers grow at a 47 percent clip in the past 10 years. Of the 730,000 Americans who are NAIC club members, 61 percent are women, a number that was unthinkable in 1960, when I joined a club. Then 90 percent of NAIC members were men. Participants are getting younger as well: the average age of investment club members is now 48, down from 60 in 1988. Better yet, NAIC studies show that within five years of joining an investment club, members of all ages wind up investing three times as much of their own money in the stock market as they do in their club's investments.

Club Rules

Usually made up of groups of neighbors, coworkers, family, or friends—or a mixture of each—and averaging about 15 members per club, investment clubs are formed to pool money among club members and invest that money in the group's best recommendations. They meet in church basements, neighborhood pubs, each other's houses, or, for some of the larger clubs, in hotel banquet rooms. Typical monthly dues range anywhere between $25 and $100. Many clubs place strict limits on what types of stocks they can buy (some don't invest in nuclear power or military defense companies; others avoid alcohol and/or tobacco companies) and on how much they'll spend per share. Some clubs will place a limit of $40 or $50 per share of a stock and not exceed it. If you want to spend $100 on a share of stock, you may go right ahead—on your own.

Each month a different group member or members is given the assignment to research the four or five stocks suggested at the last month's meeting. That way, every club member learns how to evaluate a company's financial fortunes and keep a critical, objective eye on factors like company profits, price-to-earnings ratios, and dividend yield. If nothing else, investment clubs are great training grounds for serious stock market investing.

Once a decision to buy a stock is made, a portion of the dues goes into the new stock. There's very little market-timing going on—the NAIC reports that the average investment club members hang onto their stock for 7 years. Brokerage companies hate that, and they hate investment clubs in general. Anything that teaches novice investors about the financial markets is viewed by brokerage houses as detrimental to their potential profits. That's why many investment club stock transactions are executed by discount brokers or via the Internet.

There are a few things you ought to know before joining an investment club. The first is to be serious about your commitment. Club members are no-nonsense investors who might look askance on someone they feel isn't pulling his or her own weight. If you travel a lot on your job you may wind up missing a lot of club meetings and ticking your associates off.

Evaluate your risk/reward parameters. Some investors prefer mutual funds because they don't have to make the actual investment decisions—that's what they're paying the fund manager to do. Typically, investment clubs don't bother with conservative investments like bonds or money market securities. So if you're skittish about pouring money every month into the stock market, maybe an investment club isn't the right venue for you.

Overall, investment clubs are a great idea for novice investors. By joining, you'll learn the importance of investing regularly, regardless of how the markets are doing, and master the discipline of reinvesting dividends and capital gains. Peer pressure is a wonderful incentive to resist the temptation of taking dividends or capital gains and buying yourself a new set of golf clubs. Best of all, investment clubs are a great way to learn about the stock market. And everything you learn about investing—wherever you learn it—will enable you to work with your 401(k) plan more effectively. Which is why we're here.

Knute's Knotes

Investment Fraud: The Top Abuses

Part of learning more about investing is knowing when a potential investment doesn't pass muster. According to the North American Securities Administrators Association, here are the top 10 areas of investment fraud. If you come across one, turn back. If you have to invest in any of them, proceed carefully.

1. *Affinity group fraud.* Investment scams targeting religious, ethnic, and professional groups, perpetrated by members of the groups or people claiming to want to help them.
2. *Internet fraud.* Scams using the Internet that include stock-price manipulation, illegal pyramid schemes, and insider trading.
3. *Abusive sales practices.* Sales of securities to investors who can't afford them; fraudulent securities offerings; market manipulation.
4. *Investment seminars.* Regulators are monitoring the proliferation of investment seminars and financial planners, watching for unlicensed activities and hidden fees and commissions.
5. *Telemarketing fraud.* High-pressure telephone operations.
6. *Municipal bonds.* Risky municipal bonds secured by overvalued real estate that are marketed as "safe."
7. *Immigration investments.* Sales of investments portrayed as conferring "alien immigration status" on foreign nationals.

8. *Bogus franchise offerings.* Fraudulent franchise investments, often sold at business opportunity and
   franchise shows.
9. *High-tech products and services.* Misleading or illegal sales of high-tech investments with promises of
   high profits and minimal risk.
10. *Entertainment deals.* Scams touting investments in
    movie and entertainment deals, with promises of
    guaranteed profits and failure to disclose risks.

So buyer beware. If an investment sounds too good to
be true, it probably is.

The Ins and Outs of Investment Newsletters

Unlike investment clubs, which emphasize team play and an all-for-
one, one-for-all group mentality, investment newsletters are geared toward rugged individualists. No need to bring a pot of chili or a good
bottle of wine to a club meeting or bother to dress up. With an investment newsletter, you can kick off your shoes, prop your feet up on the
couch, and open a beer as you peruse the latest investment newsletter.

The larger questions with investment newsletters are: Can you count
on them at all and which ones are best? We'll get to these questions in a
moment, but first let's take a look at what an investment newsletter is,
what it offers, and how much cash it's going to set you back.

Investment newsletters cover financial markets of all stripes:
stocks, bonds, mutual funds, options, precious metals, even orange juice
futures. Newsletters vary in length from 4 to 20 pages and are usually
mailed monthly or quarterly right to your home (or, in recent years,
electronically via the Internet). One thing you'll learn quickly about
such newsletters is that they aren't free. Every newsletter publisher
thinks he's got the greatest financial mind since J.P. Morgan and is

reluctant to provide any insights without an ample fee. Subscriptions to investment newsletters can between $25 and $500 annually.

Unfortunately, newsletter publishers are unregulated. So you have to be careful when choosing one. Most newsletter producers will gladly send you a sample issue free of charge, so you can kick the tires a bit. Anyone who isn't willing to give you a free sample likely has something to hide.

One objective source for investment newsletters is *Hulbert's Financial Digest*, a "newsletter about newsletters" that monitors about 500 investment newsletters and tracks their performance. Founder and publisher Mark Hulbert warns that only 20 percent of investment newsletters actually make money for their readers. Hulbert says that two factors weigh heavily in identifying those 20 percent. First, look at the 5-year track record of the newsletter. Second, examine the risk associated with its investment portfolio. All things being equal, if you have to choose between two newsletters offering similar performance, take the one with less risk. The riskier newsletter's portfolio being more volatile, it will be difficult for it to produce consistently good returns over time.

Knute's Knotes

Ranking the Newsletters

Want a peek at what the professionals consider the best investment newsletters? According to *Hulbert Financial Digest*, here are the top producers, based on the performance of the newsletter's model portfolio. Benchmark criteria come from the Wilshire 5,000 stock index, with ranking of 100 or more meaning that the newsletter's portfolio has outperformed the Wilshire index and rankings under 100 meaning that they have underperformed the Wilshire index.

Top 5 Newsletters for the 10-Year Period Ending November 30, 1997

Newsletter	10-Year Annualized Return	Risk-Adjusted Rating	Phone
Performance Only			
1. *OTC Insight*	29.7%	78.1	(800) 955-9566
Recommends high-performance small-capitalization stocks.			
2. *Prudent Speculator*	27.7%	79.1	(714) 497-7657
Pursues a value-oriented stock-picking approach, frequently augmented by the use of margin or leverage.			
3. *MPT Review*	26.6%	84.2	(800) 454-1395
Recommends high-performance small-capitalization stocks.			
4. *New Issues*	22.7%	89.4	(800) 442-9000
Hunts for bargains among initial public offerings.			
5. *BI Research*	21.2%	73.6	(203) 270-9244
Applies a value-oriented stock-picking approach to relatively unknown small companies.			
Wilshire 5,000	18.2%	100.0	
Risk-Adjusted Rating			
1. *Fidelity Monitor*	18.2%	106.2	(800) 397-3094
Focuses on mutual funds offered by Fidelity Investments, using a value-oriented selection process.			
2. *No-Load Fund Investor*	14.0%	100.3	(800) 252-2042
Provides commentary and recommendations on commission-free mutual funds.			
3. *Fundline*	18.4%	100.0	(818) 346-5637
Uses technical analysis to advise on trading mutual funds.			
4. *Investment Quality Trends*	15.0%	91.1	(619) 459-3818
Recommends large-capitalization stocks that pay relatively generous dividends.			
5. *New Issues*	22.7%	89.4	(800) 442-9000
Wilshire 5,000	18.2%	100.0	

Source: *Hulbert Financial Digest.*

Get Smart

On Wall Street, knowledge is power. That's why reading solid newspapers like *The Wall Street Journal, Barron's, Investor's Business Daily*, and *USA Today* can provide a significant boost to your 401(k) investment strategy. Also check out the financial pages of your local newspaper. They're especially useful in researching local companies. Make it a point to browse through some financial magazines, too. Like investment newsletters, most magazine publishers will offer you at least one issue free for you to sample. My personal favorites are *Smart Money, Money, Worth*, and *Your Money*. There are a lot of great magazines out there to choose from, depending on your area of interest.

For readers who don't have access to the Internet, a great resource free of charge is "A Guide to Understanding Mutual Funds," published by the Investment Company Institute. They'll ship you one if you call (202) 326-5800.

Remember, 401(k) millionaires are made, not born. Just like any other endeavor, a little education goes a long way.

Knute's Knotes

Six Good Books on Money and Investing

Each of these books is clearly and concisely written and can be found at your nearest bookstore or Amazon.com if you frequent the Internet. Each also deserves a spot on your bookshelf. They're already on mine.

1. *One Up on Wall Street* (Penguin USA, 1990), by Peter Lynch: Wall Street according to Lynch, the legendary Fidelity Investments money manager who built the Magellan Fund into the largest mutual fund in the world.

Another Lynch classic, *Beating the Street* (Fireside, 1994), provides readers with Lynch's tried-and-true strategies for picking winning stocks.

2. *A Random Walk Down Wall Street* (W. W. Norton & Company, 1996), by Burton G. Malkiel: A great book on stock investing. Malkiel is a jewel of a writer and an even better stock market analyst.

3. *The Hulbert Guide to Financial Newsletters* (Dearborn, 1993), by Hulbert Financial Digest: The last word on investment newsletters. If you're wondering whether an investment newsletter is right for you, this is the perfect book to tell you what you need to know.

4. *Finance and Investment Handbook* (Barrons, 1998), by John Downes, Elliot Goodman, and Jordan E. Goodman: This updated classic contains everything you need to know about the financial markets and how to invest can be found here. Includes the best dictionary of investment terms (3,000 of them) I've ever seen.

5. *Warren Buffett: The Making of an American Capitalist* (Doubleday, 1996), by Roger Lowenstein on billionaire Buffett, one of the best stock-pickers ever.

6. *Bogle on Mutual Funds* (DTP, 1994): Vanguard Group Founder John Bogle expounds on his theories on mutual fund investing. If you could have only one book on mutual funds, this should be it.

Cyber School

When it comes to finding quick, useful information on investing, there's nothing like the World Wide Web. The following sites are great for novice investors who want to learn more about the financial markets in a low-pressure, no-sales pitch fashion:

1. The Securities Industry Association (www.sia.com): A good, no-holds-barred look at investment fundamentals. The information is clear, precise, and user-friendly. The site is chock full of data on new trends, like changes in Social Security and the pros and cons of the Roth IRA. But it also offers ample information on investment basics, like risk/reward and asset allocation.

2. The Mutual Fund Education Alliance (www.mfea.com): You say you don't like the advertising-heavy, buy-now-or-you'll-regret-it Web site approach of most brokerage houses and mutual fund firms? Try the MFE's Web site, which is sponsored by no-load mutual fund companies but whose charter is to provide good, solid fund investment information with no pressure. There are no ads—just screen after screen of useful fund investment basics.

3. American Online's Sage School (AOL Keyword: Personal Finance): It's presented in a fresh, clever way, with plenty of facts and figures to support the text. The site's producers had it right when they called Sage the place "where the love of investing meets the love of learning." Sage will show you what a fund is, how it operates, and present several scenarios on how to select one. Plus, it's got a great investment glossary.

4. Mutual Fund Interactive (www.brill.com): Another lively, cleanly presented mutual fund investing Web site geared toward investors looking to choose the right fund. The site offers expert market commentary from some of the best money managers around and includes fund recommendations from key investment industry analysts. It has a link to other investment-oriented Web sites like Bloomberg Online to provide you with up-to-date market activity and financial news.

5. The Motley Fool (www.fool.com): A highly engaging, chat-heavy place for cyber-investors to hang out and swap tips and scoops on the latest and greatest investment ideas. Everything from how to beat the Dow Jones Average to when to cash out on your retirement plan is covered Some of its advice from participants make its name apt, so consider the source when you log on. But it's one of the most fun, high-energy places to visit on the Web.

A 401(k) Makeover

Name: Valerie S.

Age: 35

Occupation: Pet shop manager

Retirement Goals: Earn enough from my Social Security and my 401(k) to retire on comfortably, I hope, by the age of 65.

401(k) Assets: $46,350

Portfolio: 10% Growth and income fund IRA
20% Life insurance company annuity
20% Aggressive growth fund
20% Mid-cap equity fund
30% Equity index fund

Stocks: Pfizer, Philip Morris, America Online

Comments: I've really stepped up my annual 401(k) savings, from $972 per year five years ago to three times that today. I know I need to catch up since I didn't start until my late 20s, but I like the results I've seen so far. I'm tempted to invest overseas, especially since I've been hearing about the new European common currency coming out in 1999. Europe sounds like a good place to invest to me.

Knute Says

Europe is a great place to invest—today. Yesterday, Russia was great, the day before Japan was the place to be. For a diverse portfolio, global investing is a must, but leave the investing to the professionals; use mutual funds as your international investing vehicle. Looking at your portfolio, it seems you are investing in the strategy-of-the-day. Your aggressive growth fund and your life insurance annuity are completely different animals. You need to follow the rules (start early; max out; educate yourself; be aggressive; and keep the money working). And you need to rejigger your portfolio along these lines: change your growth and income fund to a European stock fund and cash out your annuity (you may have to do this over several years in order to avoid penalties) and put it into a real estate investment trust fund (REIT). Leave everything else the same. Put any new money into a large cap stock fund until everything is about equal.

10

> *Go for the moon—if you don't get
> it, you'll still be heading for a star.*
> —Willis Reed

Be Aggressive: Your
Retirement Depends on It

You've heard me harp about the importance of investing early. And you know by now that younger investors have the significant advantage of time on their side. By investing aggressively in growth, international, or other fast-moving stock funds, they can earn sparkling returns year after year after year, and leave it to compound interest to work its annual miracles. Even when markets decline, as they periodically do, younger investors have time to recover from market corrections.

But I've got good news for you more seasoned folks, too. Investors of any age can benefit from a healthy dose of forward-looking, actively managed stock funds in their 401(k) plan. Let's face it, inflation isn't going away, and Social Security may be (baby boomers are owed $9 trillion more in Social Security payments than the next generation is currently obliged to pay in Social Security taxes). A portfolio stocked with treasury bills or money market funds will most assuredly jeopardize your chances of meeting your long-term financial goals. To pick up the slack, to keep ahead of inflation, and to protect yourself from any elimination or diminishment of Social Security, it pays to be aggressive.

That's why I love stocks—they offer you the best chance of securing a comfortable financial future and becoming a 401(k) millionaire. Over time, stocks have outperformed other investments by a wide margin. You simply can't be an aggressive investor and not emphasize stocks

Knute's Knotes

Stock Market Snapshots

When it comes to the stock market, the numbers really do tell the story. Here are some key facts and figures about the stock market that you may not know (through December 31, 1997):

Number of domestic stock exchanges: 8—New York (2), Boston, Cincinnati, Chicago, Philadelphia, San Francisco, Los Angeles. Another exchange, NASDAQ, provides stock info to brokers and dealers.

- Number of Americans who own stocks: 100 million
- Number of publicly held companies: 8,500
- Price of a seat on the New York Stock Exchange: Between $1.25 million and $1.45 million
- Average distance a floor broker walks every day on the NYSE: 12 miles
- New cash flowing into stock funds in 1997: $231 billion
- Number of shares traded daily: 600 million
- Value of shares traded daily: $26 billion
- Projected mutual fund assets through 1998: $5 trillion
- Number of years it took fund industry to reach $2.5 trillion in assets: 70 years (1920 to 1994)
- Number of years it took fund industry to add $2.5 trillion more: 4 years (1994 to 1998)
- Average annual growth of S&P 500 stock index: 1926 to 1997: 11%
- Average annual growth of S&P 500 stock index: 1977 to 1997: 16%

Source: *Seattle Times.*

in your portfolio. It doesn't matter much if you invest in large-company stocks, small-company stocks, or international stocks, just as long as you're investing in stocks. They're the foundation on which my fourth rule of 401(k) investing—being aggressive—is built. This chapter will show you how an aggressive 401(k) portfolio crammed full of stocks can translate into $1 million or more in retirement.

Invest Early and Invest in Stocks

Stocks are your best chance to combat the triple threat of inflation, investment fees, and taxes and retire comfortably. In fact, stocks have bested any other investment vehicle on earth over the years. From January 1, 1925, through December 31, 1996, when the people who keep track of such things started recording market performance, stocks overall have averaged 10.8 percent annually compared to 5.2 percent for long-term government bonds, 3.7 percent for Treasury bills, and an average annual inflation rate of 3.2 percent.

There's no doubt that stocks are the best weapon in your 401(k) arsenal. And the longer your time horizon for investing in stocks, the greater your chance for producing positive returns. With time on your side, short-term ups-and-downs in the stock market can be easily ridden out with little or no damage to your long-term investment performance:

THE CASE FOR EQUITIES:
GROWTH OF $100 FROM 1926–1996

Equity	December 31, 1925	December 31, 1996	Average Rate of Return
Stocks	$100	$137,170	10.8%
Bonds	100	3,449	5.15
T-Bills	100	1,355	3.8
Inflation (Based on Consumer Price Index)	100	889	3.2%

Although stocks may act like a rollercoaster from time to time, combining them with a long investment-time horizon can yield some amazing gains. The next chart shows how stocks almost always make money for investors (based upon the Standard & Poor's 500 Index) for various holding periods from 1928 through 1996. Take note of how the value of stocks grows the longer you hold them in your portfolio.

PERCENT OF TIME THAT STOCKS HAVE PROVIDED POSITIVE RETURNS

Holding Period:	1 Year	3 Years	5 Years	10 Years	15 Years	20 Years
	71%	87%	92%	98%	100%	100%

Source: Towers Data. Period ends December 31, 1996.

Imagine that! Not only do stocks grow in value the longer you hold them, but after 15 or 20 years, in the collective sense, *all* of the stocks you own make money. Now that's performance!

A Word on Risk

As much as I encourage investors to bulk up their 401(k)s with fast-growing stock funds, I'd be remiss in not explaining that many growth stock funds are considered high-risk investments by investment experts. American Heritage Fund, 1997's top-performing equity fund, posted 75 percent gains for its shareholders during the year. But the fund keeps only 15 stocks in its portfolio, virtually all of them volatile pharmaceutical and biotechnology companies with high risk-reward ratios. In the fund's advertisements, manager Heiko Thieme tells investors "Don't invest in my fund! If volatility and aggressive investing makes you nervous, the American Heritage Fund is not for you!"

You've got to admire that kind of candor. But Mr. Thieme knows of what he speaks. After recording a whopping 95 percent gain in 1991, the fund backtracked over the next several years, recording losses of 35 percent in 1994 and 31 percent in 1995. All in all, if you stuck with the fund over the years, you'd still come out on top. But you would have experienced one heck of a ride.

The rule I like to apply when investing aggressively is this: If you can withstand a drop of 10 percent in your portfolio without blinking an eye, and a 30 percent decline in the stock market in a single year without gagging, you'll do just fine. I remember the stock market losing 48 percent of its value in 1973–1974. It wasn't pretty, and nobody was thrilled about it. But I for one kept right on investing in stocks. In fact, the prices were so low there were some real bargains to be had during those two years.

Knute's Knotes

Addition by Subtraction? Maybe Not

There's no shortage of 401(k) investment formulas out there. If I had a nickel for every "get-rich-in-a-hurry" blueprint, I'd be a 401(k) millionaire twice over.

One formula I run into quite often is the "100-minus-your-age" asset allocation formula, designed to keep you in the right mix of stocks and bonds: You take your age and subtract it from 100.

What's remaining is what percentage of your total investments (stock market, annuities, real estate, etc.) you should invest in stocks. For example, 40-year-old Kathy subtracts her age from 100, giving her 60. That number reflects the percentage (60%) of stocks she should have in her 401(k) plan. At age 61, that number falls to 39 percent, and so on. Again, the theory is that the younger you are, the more aggressive you can be with your retirement assets. And stocks represent the most aggressive investment vehicles out there. But even those investors who subscribe to this formula to determine their asset allocation—a practice that I wholly endorse, by the way, for the risk-averse—are penalized by progressively moving away from stocks in their 401(k) portfolios.

What if you ignored the 100 minus your age rule and plowed virtually all of your money into stocks? Historically, you'd hit a home run. Here's how:

> 25-year-old Jennifer is very excited about her new job at a big graphics design company. Its 401(k) plan is sensational, offering her a wide variety of investment options. Jennifer subscribes to the 100-minus-your-age rule. Right now, that means a 75 percent stock weighting for Jennifer. But by playing the subtraction game, when Jennifer reaches age 65 she'll only have 35 percent in stocks—the 40 years between age 25 and age 65 will reduce her original 75 percent stock position by one percentage point annually. According to Ibbotson Associates, a financial consulting firm, Jennifer will still do very well when she retires: she'll earn $2.9 million from her 401(k) plan alone.
>
> But she could have done even better. Imagine if Jennifer had taken her original stake at age 25 and plowed 90 percent of it into stocks and held her ground for 40 years. With the 90 percent position in stocks remaining at age 65, Ibbotson says Jennifer would have earned $3.6 million after 40 years.
>
> That's a lot of art supplies for all those beautiful vistas she'll be painting in her retirement years.

Here are some quick tips on investing in growth stocks:

1. *Buy solid companies that have some sort of track record.* The biggest mistakes in growth investing are when companies with inexperienced management and no history of profits are added to a portfolio.
2. *Be down to earth.* Don't bother with sexy-sounding initial public offerings (IPOs) or get involved with rumors about who's

taking over what. Just stick with the fundamentals like low debt and high earnings and you'll do fine.

3. *No "get rich quick" schemes.* When you find a good up-and-coming growth company or growth fund, hang on to it and give it a chance to appreciate. If you turn the investment over before it has a chance to realize the potential you saw in it in the first place, you'll probably regret it.

Shopping for Value

Value stocks are a tad different than growth stocks. Shopping for value companies is like going to the mall and seeing if you can't buy a hammer worth $10 for $7 or a dress worth $50 for $35. Professional money managers like value stocks because they represent solid companies that are undervalued by the market. Reasons for valued stocks' undervalued status are usually fleeting, like a bad quarter or questionable management, things that are corrected over time. They can thus make more money by buying companies whose assets are worth more than the company's stock price and eventually selling when the rest of the market wakes up and recognizes the true value of the company.

Unfortunately, value stocks don't come with a crystal ball. It's very difficult to figure out when a company's value is underrepresented in the market. One rule I use when evaluating value stocks is to determine whether the company could raise a lot of cash if it needed capital in a hurry. The formula for determining this is straightforward: Subtract all short- and long-term debts from company assets like cash, securities, and product inventory. If the working capital of the stock you're evaluating is at 25 percent or more than the current price, you've got yourself an undervalued stock.

For the most part, I'd leave the stock-picking to the professionals. Trying to gauge when a stock is undervalued before everyone else realizes the same thing is no mean feat. But a well-stocked value mutual fund managed by a strong, experienced stock picker is a valuable addition to any 401(k) portfolio.

Knute's Knotes

When It Gets to $100, Sell!

One revolutionary way to include individual stocks—and not only stock funds—in your 401(k) portfolio is through a new-fangled device called a 401(k) brokerage account. These accounts enable 401(k) plan participants to buy individual stocks through their 401(k) plan. Traditionally employers offered 401(k) investors many options that were limited to mutual funds. Now plan participants who fancy themselves stock-pickers can designate a portion of their plan proceeds for shares of stock in companies they like. Plan providers like Merrill Lynch or Charles Schwab execute trades on behalf of 401(k) investors for a fee.

While brokerage accounts are a mere blip on the 401(k) radar screen today (only 4% of companies offered them by mid-1998), that could change in a New York minute. Companies are constantly combing Wall Street for ways to increase the already formidable amount of individual responsibility workers have toward their own retirements.

Concerned that workers aren't savvy enough to make their own individual stock choices, however, some companies impose limits on 401(k) brokerage activity. Weston Paper in Terre Haute, Indiana, limits workers to 50 percent of total 401(k) account activity in brokerage trades.

Responding to the trend, financial services giant Charles Schwab has opened a 401(k) brokerage service with about 40 companies signed up as of mid-1998, with a total of 10,000 401(k) brokerage accounts in all. For a fee of $100 per year and about $40 per trade, the Schwab service isn't cheap. But if you've already got $100,000 or so in your 401(k) account, you could easily absorb such fees.

If, that is, you prove to be an adept stock-picker. Wall Street's concrete canyons are littered with the bones of investors who called themselves stock-pickers. So be careful about 401(k) brokerage accounts.

Have Portfolio, Will Travel: Investing Internationally

I haven't traveled much overseas, but my portfolio has. The rewards of investing overseas have been ample with or without me around. I've always made it a habit to invest internationally, and I think you should, too. Many people I know think the world begins in New York and ends in Los Angeles, and everything in between is all that matters.

Knute's Knotes

Foreign Powers

Notwithstanding the sometimes rocky ride with international stocks lately, business is booming . . . not only here in the United States but abroad. In fact, most of the world's largest companies are outside the United States. On foreign shores you'll find:

- 9 of the 10 largest electronic companies
- 8 of the 10 largest automobile companies
- 8 of the 10 largest steel companies
- 7 of the 10 largest banks
- 5 of the 10 largest chemical companies

Source: Morgan Stanley Capital International (through 1996).

That's pure bunk. Did you know that nearly two-thirds of the world's stock is in companies outside the United States? And that, historically, returns from foreign stocks have exceeded those of U.S. stocks?

After World War II and right on to the early 1980s, the United States dominated the world's economic landscape. In 1970, America's gross national product comprised almost half of the entire world's output. By 1996, however, that number had fallen to one-third.

The world's financial markets reflected the same pattern. In 1970, the U.S. stock market made up two-thirds of the world's equity market capitalization (the amount of money in stock markets worldwide). Today, that amount has declined to less than one-half of stock market assets. Economists point to international regions like Southeast Asia and Latin America, where population growth is two to three times that of the Western world. Free markets in those regions have produced an economic boom, where a new global middle-class of consumers is growing, anxious to buy their first Toyotas, townhouses, and tennis rackets.

Advocates of foreign stocks say the exposure to different economies worldwide provides more opportunities for investment profit. Plus diversifying internationally gives investors some protection against a domestic bear market, like the one the United States saw in the early 1970s, or a severe market dip, like the ones the United States saw in 1987, 1997, and 1998. Critics of foreign stocks maintain that domestic companies like IBM, McDonald's, and Coca-Cola have blossomed overseas, thus giving U.S. investors in their stocks a significant foreign exposure. That's not, however, the same as investing in a foreign company.

If you do decide to invest some of your 401(k) money overseas, there's no lack of mutual funds to accommodate you. Hundreds of foreign funds are available to U.S. investors that provide profit opportunities overseas. These include:

- *Global Funds:* Funds that invest in both U.S. and foreign companies.
- *International Funds:* These funds invest strictly in foreign markets, and don't include U.S. stocks.
- *Regional Funds:* These funds specialize in specific geographical areas, like Western Europe, Southeast Asia, or Latin America.

- *Country Funds:* These funds also invest in specific regions, but only in specific countries within those regions, like the UK, Brazil, or Australia.

U.S. VS. FOREIGN STOCK MARKET ASSETS: 1970 AND 1996

	(In $ Billions)	
	1970	1996
Total Stock Market Assets	$929	$15,115
United States (Total Assets)	613 (66%)	6,802 (45%)
Foreign (Total Assets)	316 (34%)	8,313 (55%)

Source: Morgan Stanley Capital International.

Although the stats for the wild worldwide markets in 1998 may turn this trend upside-down, most recent years, as the world has seen its economies and financial markets expand, foreign stocks have generally outperformed their American counterparts.

In nine rolling 10-year periods from 1978–1988 through 1986–1996 show that foreign stocks cumulatively top U.S. stocks, period after period:

10-Year Periods Ended	Cumulative 10-Year Returns in U.S. Dollars	
	Foreign	U.S. Stocks
12/88	660%	350%
12/89	715	405
12/90	400	395
12/91	450	400
12/92	405	365
12/93	415	300
12/94	425	285
12/95	275	295
12/96	115	310

True, foreign stock performance tails off by 1996 (and decidedly more so in 1997, when markets in Southeast Asia were roiled). But with a roaring European economy in 1998, bolstered by the single European currency due out in January 1999, many financial experts say Europe is the place to be for stock investors at the end of the twentieth century.

And overall, according to the Morgan Stanley Capital International (MSCI) Europe Australasia Far East (EAFE) Index (the global version of the U.S.'s Standard & Poor's 500 Index), foreign stocks outperformed U.S. stocks in 14 of the previous 16 ten-year periods ending in 1996.

The beauty of international mutual fund investing through your 401(k) plan is that you don't have to muck about calculating currency

Knute's Knotes

The World's Top Market Performers, 1982–1996

During the 15-year period from 1982 through 1996, the U.S. stock market ranked number one overall in the world a single time—way back in 1982. Here's a list of the winners:

Year	Best Market	U.S Rank Among 11 Major Markets
1996	Hong Kong	5
1995	Switzerland	2
1994	Japan	7
1993	Hong Kong	10
1992	Hong Kong	3
1991	Hong Kong	3
1990	United Kingdom	4
1989	Germany	4
1988	France	8
1987	Japan	6
1986	Japan	9
1985	Germany	6
1984	Hong Kong	4
1983	Australia	7
1982	United States	1

Source: Morgan Stanley Capital International; Frank Russell.

rates and deciding whether that Italian jewelry manufacturer should claim a spot in your portfolio. Your fund manager takes that responsibility for you.

A core international fund with a broadly diversified stable of stocks should fit the bill nicely for most 401(k) investors. If you like a particular region, like Europe or Southeast Asia, plenty of region-specific mutual funds are available.

And if your company doesn't offer an international mutual fund option in your 401(k) plan, stomp your feet and raise the dickens. These days, no 401(k) plan should be without some international flavor. *Diversification is your goal—It will increase your return while reducing your risk.*

Active Versus Passive Investing: Gung-Ho or Ho-Hum?

Many perfectly reasonable, level-headed people I meet tell me that index funds are the only way to go. Now don't get me wrong. I think some funds have some advantages, but in general the downside to index funds turns me off.

What is an index fund? It's the strategy of buying and holding an investment tied to a particular benchmark, or index, in roughly the same quantity as the index it's shadowing. An index mutual fund simply mirrors the investment performance of, say, the S&P 500 Index by picking the same companies that comprise the S&P 500. Then they just sit back and make do with whatever results the S&P 500 produce. Index funds are very trendy in the late 1990s, with index funds based on the Russell 2000 small stock index, and the European and Asian stock markets gaining popularity.

Indexing is what's known in money circles as "passive investing." That means very little investment strategy and very low fees for shareholders, as the companies who run index funds, like The Vanguard Group, don't shell out a lot in overhead. Theoretically, index fund managers say, the 2 percent index fund investors save in lower management fees means that active fund managers will have to outperform index funds by a 2 percent margin just to keep pace. As I said, I have no huge problem with index funds: for the last 70 years you'd have averaged 11.6 percent by investing in an S&P index fund. But that's exactly what I don't like about index funds—you're never going to do better than the S&P 500. If the rest of the world is enjoying 20 percent average returns on its stock funds and the S&P 500 is lagging at 8 percent, guess what return you're stuck with?

And when a bull market runs its course? Index funds offer you no downside protection against a downward spiral of the Dow Jones Industrial Average. Even growth fund managers deploy defensive measures in the event of a descending stock market. Index funds are locked in, like it or not. Plus, harder-to-track indices like small-cap and foreign stocks are harder to frame an index fund around. Consequently, index advocates may miss out on big years in those sectors.

FUND PERFORMANCE CHART BY CATEGORY, 1988–1998 (ON A TOTAL RETURN BASIS, DATA AS OF MAY 31, 1998)

Fund Objective	1 Year	3 Years	5 Years	10 Years
Growth and income	23.54%	25.33%	19.44%	15.86%
Equity income	20.95	23.21	17.64	14.72
Sector	17.03	22.77	18.55	18.30
Utility	25.93	19.13	12.30	13.44
Growth	25.38	24.18	19.25	16.50
Latin America	−24.20	9.09	4.60	n/a
Health & biotechnology	17.97	24.42	21.64	21.78
Small cap	18.13	20.06	16.97	15.45
Capital appreciation	22.12	21.04	16.82	15.13
Mid cap	22.22	20.63	16.95	15.85
Balanced	17.58	17.82	13.97	12.86
European region	33.0	24.03	21.18	12.4
Stock & bond funds	14.96	16.08	12.68	11.53
Science & technology	25.43	19.52	21.72	19.73
Global funds	12.88	16.91	15.12	12.14
International	8.17	12.95	12.23	10.31
Natural resources	−10.98	9.98	8.25	9.11

Fund Objective	1 Year	3 Years	5 Years	10 Years
Emerging markets	-31.86	-4.09	0.53	n/a
Pacific region	-44.97	-13.37	-5.23	1.01
Gold	-34.97	-17.10	-10.61	-3.89
High-yield taxable bond	11.44	12.36	9.93	10.3
High-yield municipal bond	9.48	7.86	6.47	7.93
General taxable bond	7.73	9.6	7.48	9.24
Long-term investment grade corporate bond	10.42	7.86	6.95	9.05
Long-term U.S. treasury/ govt. bond	10.97	7.14	6.12	8.42
General municipal debt	8.39	7.32	5.78	7.97
Single state municipal debt	8.13	7.2	5.67	7.78
Intermediate investment grade corporate bond	9.43	7.09	6.13	8.32
Intermediate term U.S. treasury/govt. bond	9.1	6.58	5.52	7.78
Short-term U.S. treasury/ govt. bond	6.52	5.79	4.94	7.01
Short-term investment grade corp. bond	6.59	6.01	5.35	6.97
World bond	3.65	8.4	5.86	7.43

Benchmarks for Mutual Fund Investors (Annualized) Investment Objective	1 Year	3 Years	5 Years	10 Years
Dow Jones investment average (w/divs)	18.68%	27.77%	23.35%	18.72%
S&P 500 (w/divs)	30.15	30.24	23.08	18.56
Small-co. index fund	16.94	20.06	17.04	13.71
Lipper index: Europe	33.88	25.19	21.2	n/a
Lipper index: Pacific	-39.43	-11.07	-4.09	n/a
Lipper L-T govt.	9.95	6.95	5.58	7.71
Avg. U.S. stock fund	22.62	23.13	18.45	15.87
Avg. Bond Fund	8.98	7.56	6.33	8.56

Source: Lipper Analytical Services.

"Actively managed" funds, on the other hand, involve a lot of buying and selling on the part of the manager, and a lot of research and analysis on the part of the manager's staff, all of which does lead to higher fees. But actively managed mutual funds are more flexible and offer greater potential return on your investment. Of course, they also offer more risk. Growth and value funds are examples of active investing. If you're an inexperienced investor who can live with lower returns with less risk, then index funds might be for you. But if you're determined to take full advantage of the historically higher performing actively managed funds like growth, value, and international funds, then the gung-ho approach is for you.

See how various fund categories performed against their benchmarks from May 31, 1988, through May 31, 1998 (pages 178–179). Note how stock funds significantly outperform their bond counterparts. Also take note of some of the higher risk investments, like Southeast Asia-oriented funds and gold funds. It's been a long ten years for investors in those sectors.

Paying Off Your Mortgage Versus Putting the Money into the Stock Market

Sometimes people come into unexpected money, like an inheritance, a big raise or bonus at work, or maybe even winning the lottery. If you receive a financial windfall, don't be tempted to try and pay off your mortgage first. Instead, consider putting the money to work for your retirement and invest it in the stock market. Here's why.

Say you have a $100,000 fixed-rate mortgage at 7 percent interest. The monthly check you cut to your bank is $665.30. One happy day you win the lottery and pocket $100,000.

If you decide to use the money to pay off the house early and invest the equivalent of your monthly mortgage check ($665.30) in the stock market, you do all right. With average annual gains of 15 percent (high historically, but not over the past few years), you'll earn $3.7 million at the end of 30 years (and you'll own your house).

Knute's Knotes

Take advantage of your longer lifespan: Keep investing when you're retired.

No matter how well you prepare for retirement, you sure could use an extra $100,000 or $200,000 when you get there. The question is how can you get it?

Easy. By continuing to invest during your golden years, you can add to your retirement largesse. The following chart shows how an investor who retired in 1975 and kept investing made out over the ensuing 20 years. Numbers are based on initial investment of $10,000 in a conservative, moderate, and aggressive portfolio, from December 31, 1975, to December 31, 1994. All dividends and interest were reinvested:

Type Portfolio	Portfolio Makeup	Return
Conservative Portfolio	20% stocks/55% bonds/25% cash	$ 69,000
Moderate Portfolio	60% stocks/30% bonds/10% cash	132,900
Aggressive Portfolio	95% stocks/0% bonds/5% cash	215,700

It's no surprise that the aggressive portfolio returned the most money by far on the original $10,000 investment. The moral of the story? Just because you're retired doesn't mean you have to stuff your 401(k) assets into a mattress, or even plow them all into a conservative, bond-laden portfolio. Stocks give you the most growth for your money.

Source: Ibbotson Associates, 1994.

But if you take the $100,000 lottery gain and invest it straight into the stock market with the same results, while still paying your monthly mortgage as you always have, you'll have $6.6 million in investment

Knute's Knotes

Mad Money: Higher Risk Ideas for the Adventurous Investor

As you grow older and find you're making even more money than you expected, don't hesitate to fulfill any secret desires to act like Warren Buffett and pick stocks like the pros. Just do it outside of your 401(k) or other retirement plan.

It's no sin to have fun investing in stocks, or even higher-risk securities like silver (one of my personal favorites), currencies, or cattle futures. Hey, even Hillary Clinton made $100,000 on cattle futures! If that's what stokes your competitive fires and makes you feel alive, do it. Obviously, read up on any investment vehicle you're not sure about.

The purpose of keeping some fun money on the side to invest with is two-fold. First, you hope to make money by doing so. Second, in order to know what's going on with your "mad" money, you need to know about the markets you're speculating in. That, in turn, gets you further in the habit of researching investment ideas and consequently makes you a smarter investor overall.

One rule for the road: Never invest more than 10 percent of your overall assets in these types of investment vehicles. They're not called risky for nothing. But once you know what you're doing, you may even make more money for your retirement out of the deal.

returns after 30 years, assuming the same 15 percent after-tax returns. And, you'll own your house.

Just because you got a late start on your 401(k) savings plan doesn't mean you shouldn't emphasize stocks in your portfolio. If you're trying to play catch-up, you need the growing power of stocks on your side in the years leading toward retirement. You late-starters have a big advantage over previous generations of savers—your good health and longevity. First consider that there hasn't been a single 15-year period since 1926 (including the Great Depression) when the S&P 500 have lost money. Then realize that American males aged 65 can expect to live until age 80 based on U.S. census numbers, while American females aged 65 can expect to live another 19 years in retirement.

Even though you didn't start saving until you were 40, the fact that you have extra time in retirement means you have that much longer to earn more money from the historically high-performing stock market. There's no rule that says you have to stop investing when you reach age 65, or whatever age you choose to retire. Keeping your money in the financial markets can keep you even more affluent in your sunset years. With a shorter term time horizon, you may want to preserve some capital and invest moderately in safer bond-oriented investments. But remember the inflation monster—its appetite is ravenous and never stops eating its way into your assets. So even in retirement it's a good idea to keep a healthy chunk of your money in income-generating stocks that return more on average than do any other investments.

A 401(k) Makeover

Name: Chuck D.

Age: 22

Occupation: Dockworker

Retirement Goals: It's still too far ahead of me to get my arms around it. I'd like to save as much money as I can with my 401(k). My father showed me how compound interest works and how investing early grows your money faster and higher. That's for me.

401(k) Assets: $2,500

Portfolio: 50 Aggressive growth
              50 S&P 500-based equity index fund

Stocks: None

Comments: I want to make the stock market work for me and stay away from conservative investments like bonds. So I'm going to really count on a growth investment strategy that leans on stocks.

Knute Says

At your age and with your outlook, you'll be sitting on top of the world before you know it. Your dad was right (and we are most of the time!) about compound interest. You have over 40 years to let your money work for you. Keep investing, keep learning, and most important of all, keep that money working. Don't cash out to buy that new car or that house and by retirement time, you'll be able to do or buy anything you want. And if the market grows as it has over the past 20 years, you may be a millionaire well before you turn 60. Keep your two funds and as you put more money into your 401(k), get more diversified. After you get above about $10,000, your portfolio should look like this:

    20% Aggressive growth fund
    20% Index fund
    20% International fund
    20% Large cap value fund
    20% REIT fund

11

America is a very consumer-oriented society. When you look at all the forces arrayed to encourage people to spend instead of save, it's a wonder that people save at all.

—Ian Traquair Ball, bankruptcy attorney

Loans and Other Strategies: Never, Ever Cash a Penny Out Before Retirement

Okay, time to take inventory. In the last few chapters we've covered four of my five golden rules: invest early, invest often, bone up on Wall Street, and be aggressive with your 401(k) investments. That leaves one rule, a rule that's certainly as important as any other rule: Don't take money from your 401(k) before you retire. Think of it as the reverse of the Nike slogan and JUST DON'T DO IT!

Let's face it: You don't pluck apples off a tree if they're not ripe yet and you don't eat a cake that's half-baked. So why would you tap into your 401(k) early? The upside is you get a momentary infusion of cash to buy whatever it is you need, and the downside is that you've permanently stunted the growth of your retirement plan (i.e., the money you're going to need to live on when the paychecks stop rolling in).

The Agony of Cashing Out Early

While I'm going to spend the bulk of this chapter haranguing you about not borrowing from your 401(k), there's another, even more

185

loopy method of taking money from your 401(k) before you retire—as an early cash distribution. Let's get that one out of the way, pronto.

U.S. Labor Department studies show that 68 percent of people over age 40 and 84 percent of those under 40 fail to roll over their 401(k) plan assets when they leave their jobs. Instead, they take the money and run.

Anyone who changes jobs and doesn't roll over the 401(k) assets into another retirement plan, who elects to keep the money instead, is being stupid. First, the investor loses an automatic 10 percent of his or her 401(k) plan assets right off the top to Uncle Sam. That's the government's cut for the investor acting rashly and cashing out early. Then, the investor has to pay taxes on the money he or she has taken out of the 401(k)—in the higher tax bracket they're in right now, and not the lower one the investor will most likely be in after retirement.

Worst of all, you take the best weapon you have in your retirement campaign—compound interest—and pour battery acid on it. I know I've said throughout this book that most workers have time on their side, but science tells us that we can't expect to live to be 150-years-old. And, believe me, that's how long it's going to take you to catch up to a 401(k) plan that has been cashed out early.

Let me end this admittedly blunt lecture against cashing out of your 401(k) plan early with a story:

There was this guy I knew named John. Unfortunately, John lost his job and had to find another one. Fortunately, John already had about $100,000 in his 401(k) plan. So all John had to do to ensure that he keep his retirement gravy train on track was to roll the money over into a tax-deferred IRA until he found a new job, where he could likely roll his money over again into his new employer's 401(k) plan. Sounds like a no-brainer, right? Not to John.

No, he elected to cash the whole shootin' match out right then and there and take his family on a cross-country trip. Not smart, John. He bought a Winnebago for $40,000 and used the rest for spending money for the year-long adventure. But things unraveled fast. First, the Winnebago developed a balky transmission after some miles on the road. Then, one of John's kids broke an ankle jumping up and down on a hotel bed while the Winnebago was in the shop. And life on the road seemed to cost a lot more than John remembered from his college days, when he had made the same trip with some friends in a beat-up Volkswagen bus for about $1,000—round trip. Factor in hotel rooms while the Winnebago was being fixed, endless meals at truckstops and roadside restaurants, admission to zoos, ballgames, beaches, and amusement parks. It all added up.

A scant 90 days after he'd started out, John looked at his bank balance and saw a disturbing figure. His $100,000 retirement nest egg had dwindled to $27,000, and the family had only traveled a third of the way cross-country.

Suddenly John didn't feel so good. He thought of the retirement money he'd squandered, and how much his 401(k) nest egg would have earned his wife and family in 35 years if he'd only kept the money working in the financial markets where it belonged. John dreamed of life in retirement, with no kids in the house, and a cross-country Winnebago trip with just him and his wife. That trip would have worked out better, especially since his $100,000 stake would have likely grown to $1 million in 25 years.

No way now, John acknowledged. Heck, he'd be lucky to retire at age 65 now, let alone have all that money for retirement.

John announced to his family that the trip was over and they were heading back home so he could find a new job. When he found that job, he announced, there'd be some belt-tightening in the household because he vowed to double his 401(k) plan contributions in his new job.

Good for John. At least he's seen the light. It may not be too late to retire comfortably, but it's an uphill fight now. All because he wanted to have now what he'd really appreciate in retirement.

Moral of the story? John's a nice guy who wanted to do well for his family. But don't pull a John. If you leave your old job and get a new one, the first thing to do, even before cleaning out your desk, is to arrange for your 401(k) plan money to be rolled over.

Hard Truths About Hardship Withdrawals

While nobody in government or in the fund industry encourages it, 401(k) bigwigs have made it possible for you to draw cash from your 401(k) plan under what is considered "hardship" circumstances. Hardship withdrawals are worse than an actual 401(k) loan in that you have to pay taxes on the amount of money you take out of your fund. As we'll see later in this chapter, that's *not* the case with 401(k) loans.

To qualify for hardship status, you must demonstrate an immediate and urgent need for funds that are unable to be raised elsewhere: Too much in life fits into the hardship category. Understandably, medical emergencies are serious business and you need to find cash for those types of situations anywhere you can, 401(k) plan included. But the government also considers a purchase of a home or college tuition bills as "hardship-worthy." Not me.

If you're that desperate for a new home, save for a down payment on one. Most home-buyers can get away with as little as 5 percent down payment on a home. College costs are better met by taking out student loans, applying for grants, or establishing a savings plan geared specifically to meeting college costs for your kids.

If you do decide to ignore my advice, Ted Benna, the founding father of the 401(k), has a good tip for hardship withdrawals made to pay for a down payment on a new house:

> If you must take the withdrawal, take it early in the year. A $20,000 down payment on your new home taken out of your 401(k) will cost you about 30 percent or 40 percent of your plan assets in overall taxes and penalties. But if you take the money in January, that gives you the whole year to reinvest in your new 401(k). At the same time, you can knock off some of the remaining debt by taking tax deductions on both mortgage interest and property taxes.

You still probably won't break even by year's end, but those moves can take some of the sting our of your hardship withdrawal.

Loan Lunacy: How to Avoid the Perils of 401(k) Borrowing

According to the Profit Sharing/401(k) Council of America, 84 percent of 401(k) plan participants have the option of borrowing up to half their total plan assets. Of those, 30 percent actually do so. The PCSA reports that loan-takers come from all walks of life, from mailroom attendants to chief executive officers.

At first glance, borrowing from your 401(k) looks easy. You're borrowing money from yourself and paying yourself back with interest at a competitive interest rate (usually a point or two above national bank prime lending rates). The loan can be handled with a single phone call to your employer, and the check can look mighty big when it lands on your desk. Payment is easy, too. It's handled through payroll deduction, just like your 401(k) contributions.

But when people drool over those big checks they get from borrowing from their 401(k) plans, they don't understand the toll that the loan will take on their retirement savings. Take away the magic of compound interest, and a $25,000 loan can cost a $50,000 401(k) account more than $10,000 in 20 years' time, even if the loan is repaid in full. Then there's the problem of equaling your preloan contributions to your 401(k) while repaying the loan you took. Most people won't like the double-whammy of loan payments *and* 401(k) contributions coming out of their paychecks. Often, they'll choose one over the other, and it's usually the 401(k) contributions that get the boot.

Taking a loan out of your 401(k)—heaven forbid—is like eating a ballpark hot dog without mustard—it just shouldn't be done. Even though it is your money, the deck is stacked against you when hitting yourself up for emergency cash.

Here are several reasons why borrowing from your 401(k) is not a good idea:

- When you borrow from your 401(k) plan, you are borrowing from pretax dollars and paying with posttax dollars. One 401(k) loan can undo years of disciplined retirement plan investing.
- Loan interest payments are not tax-deductible.
- Defaulting on your loan will result in your paying taxes on the amount and possibly incurring a 10 percent penalty from the IRS.
- The fund manager will extract a fat "administration" fee of anywhere from .5 percent of your total fund assets on up for handling the transaction. On a $100,000 401(k) plan, that's 500 bucks. All for just pushing a button on a computer and cutting you a check.
- Studies show that more than half of 401(k) investors who take loans from their 401(k) reduce or eliminate their previous rate of contributions. If you do take a loan, keep contributing to your 401(k). In fact, beef up your contributions to compensate.

Knute's Knotes

The Taxman Cometh

Perhaps the silliest fallacy of modern times is that 401(k) loans are not tax-penalized. I beg to differ.

When you retire and cash out on your 401(k) plan, you'll be taxed on the distributions. That includes taxes on interest earned from your 401(k) investments, which are as much a part of your plan as your original contributions. When you cash out your 401(k) upon retirement, the interest you paid to yourself on your loan is taxed as well.

Unfortunately, unlike 401(k) contributions, loan interest is paid on an after-tax basis and not on a before-tax basis. That means you're paying taxes twice on the money you've earned—and taken out in loans—from your 401(k) plan.

The allegedly "free" interest payments on 401(k) loans I keep hearing about are gibberish. A $6,000 loan taken from a 401(k) today and paid off over five years is going to cost you about $400 in extra income tax before the loan is completely paid off (assuming you're in the 28 percent tax bracket). In other words, you just slapped an additional 1.5 percent of additional annual interest on your 401(k) loan.

I'd walk away from a banker who offered me those loan terms. And so should you.

What if you have to change jobs? Your previous employer won't be thrilled with your leaving the company for a new one, and will likely take a less-than-friendly stance on your 401(k) loan repayment. In short, they'll want the money back fast. Usually, a former firm owed money on a 401(k) loan will simply raid the remaining 401(k) funds to pay the tab. There's no warm and fuzzy overture from an old employer saying, "Oh, don't worry about the 401(k) loan . . . pay us back when you can." Uh-uh. It doesn't work that way. Under most circumstances, if a loan isn't repaid to your old company within 60 days, the money is taken from your 401(k) not as a loan by your ex-employer, but as a lump-sum early withdrawal, complete with federal and state taxes and 10 percent slapped against you by your friends at the IRS.

A Horse of a Different Color

There's another form of 401(k) "borrowing" that's just as insidious as the traditional 401(k) loan and just as draining on your retirement savings. It's called a credit card. By mid-1998, Americans had saddled themselves with over $450 billion in credit card debt. According to Ram Research, a credit card tracking firm, consumers are paying interest on 78 percent of that debt. Most card companies, their trumped-up and transient offers of "low interest rates" notwithstanding, are charging between 17 percent and 18 percent in interest rates annually, says Ram Research.

Whoa, Nellie. If your 401(k) investments are earning you a healthy average of 15 percent annually, that figure still doesn't keep up with the 18 percent interest rate debt incurred from your credit card. There's simply no way on earth that a 401(k) investment, over the long haul, can compete with credit card rates—running a credit card balance while contributing to a 401(k) plan is a loser's game.

The moral of the story? If you have a running credit card debt and are paying 18 percent interest, take a pair of scissors and cut the card in half and throw it away. You're just going to have to cut some other household expenses and put more money toward retiring the onerous credit card debt. And whatever you do, keep contributing to that 401(k). It's still your best bet financially.

Them Borrowing Blues

When all is said and done, you know what my biggest problem is with borrowing money from your 401(k)? It's not the reduction in earning

Knute's Knotes

401(k) Credit Cards: An Idea Whose Time Should Never Come

An idea right up there with the Edsel and New Coke is meandering its way down to the masses. It's a 401(k) credit card.

Some banks are counting on the fact that you want to take money out of your 401(k), but you just don't have an easy way to do it. Thus they're in the banking lab right now cooking up the 401(k) Visa card.

Any bank thinking about a 401(k) credit card should be ashamed of itself. They're planning to tempt you with slightly lower interest rates, a $10,000 borrowing limit, and fast access to your 401(k). But the downside is severe. Unlike traditional 401(k) loans, where your loan payments are automatically deducted from your paycheck, you have to physically write a check to the bank at the end of each month to make good on your 401(k) credit card distributions. That's just one more bill to throw on the pile, next to the utility, phone, and cable bills. And that makes it easier to default on your 401(k) withdrawals and your 401(k) credit card. Remember, default triggers taxes on outstanding loans. Plus, there's always that high interest rate to account for. Even though participating banks say that they will cut 401(k) card rates from 18 percent or 19 percent to about 12 percent, that's still a lot of additional money to pay to gain access to your 401(k).

An old boss once told me that American consumers always get what they want. I think 401(k) credit cards will be in the category of "be careful what you wish for."

power, the tax woes, or the burdensome administration fees associated with the loans, although they all drive me batty.

No, the simple, fundamental flaw in borrowing from a 401(k) is that it turns you from a long-term financial planner into a short-term opportunist. When you take a loan from your retirement plan, you no longer see your 401(k) plan as your retirement motherload, you see it as an ATM machine. Hello, Nordstrom's, good-bye comfortable retirement.

The sad truth is that as 401(k) loans have become easier to get, the use of such loans is on the rise. In 1992, only 23.6 percent of 401(k) participants had outstanding loans from their 401(k). The average balance was $4,400. By 1996, those numbers rose significantly. Over 28 percent of 401(k) users had loans outstanding, while their balances rose to $5,537.

I hope I can convince you not to become one of those statistics. Your retirement is riding on the notion that you won't get sidetracked and take money from your 401(k). I don't think it's an understatement to say that your financial future is at stake. If you can keep your fingers out of the 401(k) cookie jar until retirement, you'll be amply rewarded.

If you can't, then start trying on those fishnet hats and oversized aprons you see at the local fast-food joint. Because that could be your financial future.

A 401(k) Makeover

Name: Maryanne C.

Age: 38

Occupation: Bank supervisor

Retirement Goals: I'd like to retire early at about age 55 and spend time with my grandkids (I've got a four-year-old girl and two-year-old boy right now). If I can make $1 million for retirement, that would be great! I just hope that $1 million 20 years from now will actually mean something!

401(k) Assets: $290,000

Portfolio: 60% Growth stock fund
20% High-yield bond fund
10% Corporate bond fund
10% Money market fund

Stocks: Walt Disney, Liz Claiborne, Lucent Technology

Comments: To me, there's a big difference between saving and saving to invest. When I was 20 years old, my philosophy used to be "let me save so I can spend." But that's not what investing is all about. You need to tie in to a larger theme, like college savings, a new house, or your retirement. Once you learn to save for the long-term, the rest is easy.

Knute Says

You've made a great start and you're well on your way to becoming a 401(k) millionaire if you keep it up. And with two children and all those grandkids you've got on your mind, spending that million will be even easier. Since you have 15 to 20 more years to invest, I suggest that you become more aggressive with your holdings and more diversified. Eliminate the bond funds and the money market fund and divide the money into an international fund and an index fund. Then divide your growth stock fund into three equal parts: ⅓ into a growth stock fund, ⅓ into a large cap value fund, and ⅓ into a small cap fund. Then you'll be on the fast track.

12

90% of success is just showing up.
—*Woody Allen*

Knute's Recipe
for Success

Call me a traditionalist. I like freshly made ice tea or lemonade, but I can't stand the canned stuff. I prefer homemade blueberry pie to the frozen ones you get at the supermarket. I appreciate old-time values like paying $10 for a haircut at a place downtown with the red-and-white striped pole out front. And I prefer giving my business to a mom-and-pop diner rather than eat at one of those new chain restaurants where the menus never change and you have to wait an hour for a table on Saturday night to take your family to dinner.

But, I'm getting up there in years and I realize things change. Often, like new technologies and procedures for hospitals and more advanced school systems for our kids, change is great. As far as I'm concerned, things like e-mail and micro-brewed beer are fine.

When it comes to managing your money, though, it's the old-time fundamentals that count. Fundamentals like my five rules of 401(k) investing; investing early, investing often, learning about investing, being a confident, aggressive investor, and having the discipline to refrain from raiding your retirement fund for anything other than your retirement.

These rules mean a lot to me. That's because I know these tenets worked for my family, just as they can work for you. By building on the foundation of these five rules, you too can build a retirement portfolio that will sweep you up and carry you through your golden years in comfort and style.

Now, I know I've given you reams of advice, made many suggestions, and showed you a lot of charts, graphs, and studies and such. But one thing I haven't shown you is my own portfolio and how it's changed over the years to reflect my attitudes on investing. I think it's important for you to see firsthand how I managed my retirement savings and then let you decide if some or all of my ideas make sense for your investment style.

The difference between older investors and younger ones is the lack of information and advice we older folks received about money and investing. Sure, a lot of us had company pensions and didn't have as much responsibility as younger investors have today. But by and large we were do-it-yourselfers who had to find our own way in the world of managing money.

Just because I learned the hard way, through trial-and-error, doesn't mean you have to. I want you to learn from my experiences, from my successes and even my mistakes. In fact, that's the whole premise behind this book: to give you a 401(k) blueprint to work from, so you have a good idea of what you can expect from your retirement plan.

A big part of that process is showing you what comprises my investment portfolio today, and what comprised it throughout the various stages of my life, from young buck to proud grandfather. Along the way, I'll explain some of the investment strategies I used, like the "Dogs of the Dow," and share with you common sense notions about weathering down markets and making the most of your investment opportunities. While I consider myself a more aggressive investor than the guy next door, I think you'll find that a great deal of thought and planning went into every investment decision I made. If nothing else, it's that last point that I hope rubs off on you.

Knute's Portfolio: The Early Years

Like a superbly crafted omelet, the recipe for a successful 401(k) portfolio is deceptively simple. It doesn't matter if you're a corporate veep or a mailroom assistant. Just mix and match a few key funds and you're on your way. Here's a breakdown of my million-dollar 401(k) portfolio, starting back in 1962 with my first choices, and how I managed my 401(k) in subsequent years:

My Twenties and Thirties

Even in my younger days, when I was green around the gills money-wise, I understood that thinking long-term was going to be the frame-work of my lifetime financial plan. So even though I was prone to experimenting in faddish investment strategies like market timing and in risky investments like commodities, I was careful to always place most of my money in something reliable and sustainable, like mutual funds and tax-deferred investments.

I also learned after a while never to take money out of my so-called "retirement accounts." Common sense told me that the best crops are the ones that are left to flourish without premature harvesting: all you need is a little tending along the way (and a favorable climate doesn't hurt, either).

The third factor that has stayed with me over the years is remaining aggressive with my investments. In my 20s and 30s, I was about 100 percent invested in stocks. I joined an investment club early on to help me learn more about stocks and to get into the habit of investing on a regular basis. I also set up a budget and bought my first house in Louisville, Kentucky (for $19,000).

I made a point of investing whatever I had left over from our spending budget for the month, be it $30, $50, or $100, into a stock mutual fund. I found that the value of stock funds grew faster and higher than any other investment, and was pleased to see that as the fund grew, I could take profits out from time to time and buy 100 shares of a favorite stock. Yes, that broke the cardinal rule of raiding my mutual fund investments, but at that time there was no employer matching or tax-deferred plans, and I was young and cocky and wanted to make a quick killing in the stock market.

Boy, was I wrong. After a few years of skimming profits from my stock funds and parlaying the money into regular purchases of individual stocks, I discovered something alarming: I was still making money off the funds (even though I was pulling money out to buy stocks) and losing money on the individual stock purchases. In baseball terms, I was looking for home runs from stocks but striking out because of heavy trading costs and capital losses from my stock trades. Meanwhile, I was cracking singles and doubles with my mutual fund investments, which were really beginning to add up over the years.

So in my 30s I began to look for better-producing options than individual stocks, something fund-related that also offered me some tax advantages. That's when I first began investing in Individual Retirement Accounts (IRAs), which in turn laid the groundwork for my 401(k) investments when they came out in 1980. In the beginning, I could put $1,500 into an IRA that Uncle Sam couldn't get his mitts on, which delighted me no end. I used the money to invest in some of Fidelity Investment's stock funds, such as Magellan Fund, which was managed by a young up-and-comer named Peter Lynch.

Throughout my 30s I began maxing out as much money as I could in my Fidelity IRAs, placing the remainder of my investment money in traditional stock mutual funds. Cutting back on individual stocks and emphasizing stock mutual funds, particularly the Fidelity IRA funds, set the stage for my investment attitudes in middle age: invest in funds early and often. Oh, and I decided to keep the aggressive part, too.

My Forties

My transition into middle age coincided with a career change into sales, where for the most part I was self-employed. As any entrepreneur knows, money is tight when you first go it alone. My investments took a decidedly conservative approach during those self-employed years, with more money being poured into safer investment vehicles like certificates of deposit and money market accounts. I also started a Keogh plan—a tax-deferred investment plan for self-employed individuals. Although the need for cash was fairly constant, I wound up never taking any money out of either my Keogh plan or my tax-deferred IRAs.

As the decade wore on and I grew more stable financially, I began to dabble in some decidedly nontraditional investments like real estate and options. While I made a lot of money in some cases, I lost a lot of money in others. When the real estate market was hot in the early

1980s, I would buy a house in a new development even before it was built. After the development was finished, I would sell the house easily for a $20,000 profit without ever having to make a mortgage payment. But in the late 1980s, when the real estate market turned cold, I had to sell property I owned at 40 cents on the dollar. The same thing happened in the options market. You could make a lot of money very quickly, but you could lose it even quicker. Another valuable but expensive lesson learned: Don't invest in areas where you don't already have the knowledge or don't have the time to learn.

Fortunately, I was still maxing out on my tax-sheltered retirement plans and investing more heavily than ever in mutual funds. I moved back into the corporate world in the early 1980s and dove excitedly into my 401(k) plan, where I put the maximum amount of money I could into growth stock and growth and income mutual funds. At the time, 401(k) fund options were slim pickings. They were pretty much limited to one or two common stock funds, a fixed income fund, and a money market fund.

I also started investing in index funds, primarily from industry leader Vanguard Group, while still contributing the maximum amount of tax-deferred money allowed into my IRA plan. When the laws changed to allow spousal contributions and an extra $250 annually for married couples, I took full advantage. From 1980 to 1989, I put the allowable $250 extra into my IRA. By 1989, I had earned an extra $16,000 alone just from the IRA marriage provision. That showed me the power of compound interest, a phenomenon that has stayed with me into my retirement years.

By my late 40s, I was glad that compound interest was working in my favor. And I was doubly glad that I had started investing early to take full advantage of the magic of compound interest. With my retirement only a decade away, I was going to need all the help I could get.

My Fifties

Time to get serious. In my 50s, I took stock of how much retirement money I had accumulated. My IRAs had earned about $60,000 to that point. My mutual funds, 401(k) plan, Keogh plan, and other investments had accumulated about $250,000 more. My real estate ventures had set me back a bit, but I was able to make up a lot of ground because the stock market was performing so well in the mid-1980s.

During my 50s, I was Fidelity Investments all the time, with virtually everything tied up in Fidelity stock funds:

Growth Company Stock Fund	40%
Value Fund	10%
International Fund	10%
Canadian Fund	10%
Small Stock Fund	10%
Mid-Cap Stock Fund	10%
Junk Bond Fund	10%

My mutual fund portfolio was going great guns during that time. Twenty percent to 30 percent returns were the norm and I kept the emphasis on stock funds throughout the decade. At the time (this was the early 1990s), companies were beginning to offer 401(k) investors more fund options. But I resisted, keeping my retirement money in six mutual funds as my 60th birthday approached. Some friends of mine went whole hog and poured money into 20, even 30, mutual funds. But I've always believed you can remain diversified with as few as four to six mutual funds. I had also begun using a popular investment strategy used by many Wall Street professionals called "The Dogs of the Dow" which took advantage of buying opportunities in the Dow Jones Industrial Average, the most famous investment index in the world.

Going to the "Dogs"

Sometimes known as the "Dow Dividend Theory," the Dogs of the Dow investment strategy has roughly doubled the average annual return generated by the stock market since 1972. The idea behind the Dogs of the Dow is to buy those Dow Jones Industrial Average companies with the lowest price-to-earnings ratios and highest dividend yields. In adopting this strategy, I'm able to buy the DJIA stocks that cost the least relative to the rest of the group. The DJIA is comprised of the heaviest hitters in corporate America; companies like IBM, Exxon, and Philip Morris. Occasionally, some companies are added to the DJIA and some are dropped to make room for them.

DOGS OF THE DOW HISTORIC RETURNS: YEARLY COMPOUNDED RETURNS, 1971–1995

Year	Top 10 Dogs		DJIA		S&P 500	
	Annual Returns	Cumulative Returns	Annual Returns	Cumulative Returns	Annual Returns	Cumulative Returns
1971	4.7 %	104.7%	9.78%	109.8%	14.12%	114.1%
1972	23.32	129.1	18.18	129.7	18.72	135.5
1973	3.96	134.2	−13.16	112.7	−14.51	115.8
1974	−0.72	132.5	−23.21	86.6	−26.015	85.7
1975	56.03	206.5	44.48	125.1	36.93	117.3
1976	34.93	278.3	22.75	153.5	23.54	145.0
1977	−1.75	280.9	−12.76	134.0	−7.19	134.5
1978	−0.12	280.6	2.62	137.6	6.40	143.2
1979	12.99	315.3	10.52	152.1	18.01	168.9
1980	27.23	401.1	21.45	184.7	31.50	222.2
1981	7.73	421.3	−3.4	178.4	−4.83	211.4
1982	26.05	520.6	25.84	224.4	20.26	254.3
1983	38.75	722.2	25.68	281.9	22.27	310.9
1984	5.75	771.1	1.07	285.0	6.30	330.5
1985	29.50	1006.4	32.80	378.5	32.20	436.9
1986	32.10	1329.4	26.9	480.3	18.50	517.7
1987	6.10	1410.5	6.00	509.2	5.20	544.6
1988	26.10	1733.5	16.00	590.6	16.60	635.0
1989	26.50	2192.9	31.70	777.9	31.50	835.10
1990	−7.60	2026.2	−0.40	774.8	−3.20	808.4
1991	34.30	2822.5	23.90	959.9	30.00	1050.9
1992	7.90	3045.5	7.40	1031.0	7.60	N/A
1993	27.30	3876.9	16.80	1204.2	10.10	1244.9
1994	4.10	4035.8	4.90	1263.2	1.30	1261.1
1995	38.90	5517.0	38.60	1722.9	37.70	1736.5

Source: *Barron's*.

Every January, for example, I'd buy equal dollar amounts of the 10 DJIA stocks with the highest dividend yield. Holding these companies until the end of the year, I'd adjust my portfolio the following January to buy the current "Dogs of the Dow" crop. That way, I'd be buying good companies that had temporarily fallen out of favor and when their stock prices were low and (hopefully) selling them after they rebounded. Then I'd move on to the next batch of DJIA "Dogs." It was simple as that. In the past 10 years this strategy has earned investors 18.26 percent. From 1977 to 1997, the "Dogs" strategy only lost money three times, the worst a 7.6 percent decline in 1990.

I keep my "Dogs of the Dow" selections separate from the two primary retirement portfolios I have (described in detail later in this chapter). The reason for that is I prefer to keep my fund portfolios invested in funds and my stock portfolio invested in stocks.

That said, here's my Dogs of the Dow portfolio as of January 31, 1998:

MY CURRENT "DOGS" PORTFOLIO

Cash Value of Dogs Portfolio: $400,000

Dog Stocks: Chevron
General Motors
Minnesota Mining and Manufacturing
JP Morgan
International Paper
AT&T

Comments: Each stock represents an equal percentage of my Dogs portfolio. Over the past 20 years, my Dogs portfolio has averaged 20 percent returns, which fares well with the returns of Dogs of the Dow benchmarks over a similar time frame. In short, these Dogs may be risky, but they pay off in the end.

My Current Mutual Fund Portfolio

I'm still a big fan of the Dogs of the Dow theory, and will always make it a part of my investment portfolio. In fact, most of the strategies I've used over the years to build my retirement portfolio—an emphasis on stock mutual funds, maxing out on tax-deferred retirement plans, etc.— are still incorporated into my current investment portfolio.

True, I did grow a tad more conservative after retirement. I don't chase the "hot" mutual fund of the moment any more, preferring to invest my money in the top long-term performing mutual funds. I don't make major changes in my portfolio's asset allocation, although I almost never did in my working years, either. When it comes to picking mutual funds, I've always operated under the assumption that I've done my homework, I'm confident in the fund's objectives and its style of management, and I like its manager. So why worry about changing funds? If a fund is meeting your risk/reward objective and isn't changing its investment style, I see no reason to remove it from your retirement portfolio.

One exception is sustained underperformance. If one of my mutual funds is underperforming its industry benchmark for two years running—like a growth fund against the Standard & Poor's 500 stock index—then I'll replace the fund with another one that fits my current risk/reward parameters. But not a moment before—sometimes you're going to have to live with a slumping fund until it rebounds. Despite the bull market of the 1990s, things aren't always going to go your way as an investor. So it's best to stick with the funds you've researched and are comfortable with even if they go bad for a year or so.

Remember, your personal financial situation obviously changes in retirement. With my Social Security income, I've gained a valuable addition to my investment portfolio. I view my Social Security income as I would distributions for a bond fund. Both are fixed, both are dependable, and both provide me with a cushion to continue investing in higher returning, if riskier, stock funds. There's nothing like guaranteed income.

Another example of how your financial life changes in retirement if you planned appropriately: I don't believe I am going to outlive the money I've saved.

Consequently, I decided to divide my money in half during retirement. Half of my dual portfolio is the money my wife and I will need to live on in retirement. The other represents what I plan to leave to my kids and grandkids. Both are managed differently. (I'm taking a bit less risk with the former and more with the latter.) I know two separate investment portfolios in retirement sounds a bit offbeat. But that's okay. When you prepare for your golden years and earn $1 million or more in retirement, you'll find that you have more flexibility with your money. Being able to split my income two ways means I can take care of my current needs while ensuring that my family's future needs are attended to as well.

Let's take a look at both portfolios. The first is the conservative portfolio I'm using for my retirement income needs:

MY "CONSERVATIVE" RETIREMENT PORTFOLIO

Number of Funds: 6
Stocks: 69%
Bonds: 25%
Cash: 6%
Cash Value of Portfolio: $300,000
Funds: Gabelli Growth Fund—19%
Sound Shore Value (Large Cap) Fund—16%
Tweedy Brown American Value (Mid-Cap) Fund—15%
Cohen & Steers Special Equity (Real Estate Investment Trust) Fund—10%
Oakmark International Fund—15%
Vanguard U.S. Treasury Bond Funds—25%

Comments: I know that my definition of a "conservative" portfolio differs from that of many professional money managers. Only 25 percent of my portfolio is in bonds and the international, growth, and REIT funds represent some real risk. But as I've been saying throughout the book, an aggressive investment approach works. It keeps you ahead of inflation and provides you with superior returns. Perhaps a better definition of a conservative portfolio for me is one that's "less risky" than my aggressive portfolio. The fact is, both of my retirement portfolios rely primarily on stocks.

In my second portfolio, I'm taking a more aggressive investment approach.

MY "AGGRESSIVE" RETIREMENT PORTFOLIO

Number of Funds: 6

Stocks: 92%

Bonds: 0%

Cash: 8%

Cash Value of Portfolio: $300,000

Funds: Gabelli Growth Fund—14%
Janus 20 Fund (Large Cap Growth)—17%
Oakmark Select (Large Cap Value) Fund—26%
Baron's Small-Cap Fund—15%
Heartland Small-Cap Contrarian Fund—7%
Artisan International Fund—21%

Comments: Ironically, while this portfolio provides some welcome potential for high rates of return, by technical standards, it's not as risky a portfolio as one comprised solely of Standard & Poor's 500 Index stocks. The beta (risk) rating for the S&P index is 1.0. The rating for my current "aggressive" portfolio is only 0.9. So actually, the portfolio is less risky than your standard index fund.

You Can Do It, Too!

I've been very fortunate in life. I married a great woman, raised a wonderful family, and consider myself rich in spirit. I wouldn't change a thing. The same goes for my route to a million-dollar retirement. The value of my combined portfolios—the Dow, the conservative, and the aggressive—is a million bucks. I've had a lot of ups and downs financially over the years, and have had to learn a great deal about myself and my attitudes about money before I found the discipline and smarts to make a millionaire out of myself. But that's what makes it all so special—I found a way to save for a wonderful retirement that relied primarily on my money-management abilities, like taking an aggressive attitude toward investing, refraining from taking money out of my 401(k) early, and maxing out on my retirement plans. I received very little educational help from my employer and never relied on fancy financial advisors. All along it was just me and my family.

The best part is that you can save $1 million for retirement, too. It's so easy. You don't need anyone else's help: Just follow my five rules of retirement savings and you're on your way to the life you've always dreamed about. Believe me, I know how tough it is to sit at a desk and dream about the day you can retire. You can't wait to sail around the Bahamas, play the great golf courses of Scotland, or, in my "dream-come-true" case, open up your own seaside bed-and-breakfast. These goals are not outside your grasp! In fact, you probably don't realize how close you are to attaining them and more! Just get going and don't stop until you've realized your retirement goals.

If you're like me you'll have just as much fun making the journey as you do enjoying the fruits of your labors. It's a great trip and you'll learn a lot about yourself along the way. And when the day comes that you open up your 401(k) plan statement and see seven figures staring back at you, give yourself a pat on the back. You just became a 401(k) millionaire. Congratulations!

Appendix:
401(k) Plan Samples

Not all 401(k)s are created equal. Some are better than others and that can make a big difference in your drive for a $1 million retirement fund. Compare your 401(k) to the Fortune 500 companies listed here and measure how your company stacks up against some of the premiere companies in the United States:

Halliburton

Employees: 65,500
Participation in 401(k):   60%
When employee is eligible: Immediately
Match (per $1):   50 cents
Percent of pay matched: 4%
Maximum employee contribution: 15%
Investment options: 4
Pension plan: No
Other notes: Profit-sharing: 6 percent of pay in 1996. Company intends to improve retirement plans in 1998.

American Express

Employees: 72,299
Participation in 401(k):   75%
When employee is eligible: 1 year
Match (per $1): $1

Source: *USA Today.*

Percent of pay matched: 3%

Maximum employee contribution: 15%

Investment options: 9

Pension plan: Yes

Other notes: Profit-sharing: 4.75 percent of pay in 1996. Company also gives employees 1 percent of pay in stock. American Express is reducing its profit-sharing contributions starting in 1999.

Chrysler

Employees: 126,000

Participation in 401(k):   72%

When employee is eligible: Immediately

Match (per $1):   60 cents

Percent of pay matched: 8%

Maximum employee contribution: 20%

Investment options: 41, including lifecycle funds, plus a brokerage account

Pension plan: Yes

Other notes: Profit-sharing: $7,900 in 1996; 85 percent can go into 401(k).

Caterpillar

Employees: 57,026

Participation in 401(k):   55%

When employee is eligible: Immediately

Match (per $1):   No match

Percent of pay matched: N/A

Maximum employee contribution: Maximum allowed by law

Investment options: 10, plus a brokerage account

Pension plan: Yes

Other notes: Caterpillar also has a stock plan. Employees may contribute up to 6 percent of after-tax pay. The company matches 50 cents per $1.

Johnson & Johnson

Employees: 89,300
Participation in 401(k): 86%
When employee is eligible: 1 year
Match (per $1): 75 cents
Percent of pay matched: 6%
Maximum employee contribution: 16%
Investment options: 6
Pension plan: Yes
Other notes: N/A

PepsiCo

Employees: 140,000
Participation in 401(k): 52%
When employee is eligible: Immediately
Match (per $1): No match
Percent of pay matched: N/A
Maximum employee contribution: 15%
Investment options: 4, plus a brokerage account
Pension plan: Yes
Other notes: PepsiCo gives virtually all full-time employees stock options worth 10 percent of pay.

Gap

Employees: 66,000
Participation in 401(k): 72%

When employee is eligible: 1 year
Match (per $1): $1
Percent of pay matched: 4%
Maximum employee contribution: 16%
Investment options: 5
Pension plan: No
Other notes: N/A

Walt Disney

Employees: 117,000
Participation in 401(k):   76%
When employee is eligible: 1 year
Match (per $1):   50 cents
Percent of pay matched: 4%
Maximum employee contribution: 10%
Investment options: 8
Pension plan: Yes
Other notes: N/A

Federal Express

Employees: 99,999
Participation in 401(k):   80%
When employee is eligible: 1 year
Match (per $1):   50 cents
Percent of pay matched: N/A
Maximum employee contribution: 15%
Investment options: 7
Pension plan: Yes
Other notes: Maximum match: $500. Profit-sharing: averaged 2 percent of pay the past five years.

McDonald's

Employees: 237,000
Participation in 401(k):   95%
When employee is eligible: 1 year
Match (per $1):   50 cents
Percent of pay matched: 10%
Maximum employee contribution: 17%
Investment options: 5
Pension plan: No
Other notes: McDonald's contributed 17.15 percent of pay to profit-sharing and stock ownership plans in 1996. Employees are automatically enrolled in the 401(k); 3 percent of pay is deducted from their paychecks unless they say no.

Sears Roebuck

Employees: 300,000
Participation in 401(k):   67%
When employee is eligible: 1 year
Match (per $1):   Depends on profits; 70 cents in 1996.
Percent of pay matched: 5%
Maximum employee contribution: 17%
Investment options: 5
Pension plan: Yes
Other notes: Additional investment options planned for 1998.

MCI

Employees: 55,285
Participation in 401(k):   Declined
When employee is eligible: 3 months
Match (per $1):   67 cents

Percent of pay matched: 6%
Maximum employee contribution: 15%
Investment options: 7
Pension plan: Yes
Other notes: N/A

Investment Glossary

Becoming fluent (or at least comfortably conversational) with the financial terms listed here can help you become a more informed 401(k) investor.

Adjusted Gross Income (AGI)   The sum of annual wages, interest, dividends, capital gains/losses; less adjustments including alimony and business and moving expenses.

Advance/Decline Line   A measurement of the number of stocks that have advanced (risen in value) and the number of stocks that have declined (lost value) over a particular period. If advances outnumber the declines, it is considered a bullish trading day.

After-Tax Contribution   Money that is deducted from your paycheck and invested after taxes are withheld.

Appreciation   An increase of the value of an asset.

Arbitrage   Profiting by simultaneously buying a security in one market and selling it in another because the prices are different in both markets. By taking advantage of momentary disparities in price, the arbitrageur performs the economic function of making the markets more efficient.

Asset   Anything having value that is owned by an individual, institution, or business.

Asset Allocation   Investing in a combination of various assets or different types of investments in order to diversify and reduce the risk for optimal return.

Asked Price or Offering Price   (1) The price at which a security is offered for sale. The asked price is what the investor pays for the security. The exchange or broker-dealer or other similar entity is the seller. (2) A price at which mutual funds can be purchased. It is normally the current net asset value per sale plus sales charges if any.

Automatic Reinvestment   The program of purchasing additional shares using cash distributions and capital gain distributions usually at no or reduced cost. It is available for mutual funds and some individual securities. It allows the shareholder to accumulate capital over time using dollar-cost averaging.

Back-End Load   The redemption charge an investor pays when making a monetary withdrawal. It is usually associated with fund redemptions.

Balanced Mutual Funds   A fund that buys common stock, preferred stock, and bonds, in an effort to obtain a higher return in a lower risk strategy. It typically offers a higher yield than a pure stock fund and generally performs better when stocks are falling. However, in a rising market, the balanced fund usually does not keep pace with a pure stock fund.

Basis Point   The smallest measure used for quoting yields on bonds and notes. One basis point is 0.01 percent of yield. So, if the Federal Reserve increases rates 50 basis points, or a bond's yield changes 50 basis points, that equates to 0.5 percent.

Bear Market   Period of falling stock prices. A bear stock market usually indicates the anticipation of a declining economy. A bear bond market indicates rising interest rates.

Before-Tax Contribution   Money that is deducted from your paycheck and invested before your taxes are withheld.

Beta Coefficient   A measure of relative volatility. The Beta is the covariance of a stock in relation to the entire market. Any individual stock with a Beta greater than 1 would be more volatile than the market. Most risk-averse investors prefer stocks with Betas less than 1.

Bid or Sell Price   (1) The price at which a security is offered for purchase. The exchange, broker-dealer or other similar entity is the buyer. The bid is the price at which the investor sells the security. (2) A price at which mutual funds can be redeemed or sold. It is normally the current net asset value per share.

Blue Chip   A nationally known company with a long record of profitability, dividend payment, and with a reputation for quality. For example: General Electric, International Business Machines.

Blue-Sky Laws   Laws passed by the states to aid in protecting investors against securities fraud. The laws require sellers of new stock or mutual funds to register the offerings and provide financial data on the issues. The term is said to have originated with a judge who said that a particular stock offering he was reviewing had as much value as a patch of blue sky.

Bond   A debt security. It is usually issued by government agencies, municipalities, and corporations. The purchaser actually lends the entity money and so is considered the creditor. The entity is the seller and is considered the debtor or issuer. The issuer agrees to repay the principal amount of the loan at a specified time (maturity). Interest bearing bonds pay interest periodically at a predetermined time. A discounted bond such as a zero coupon bond pays no interest. It is sold at a discount from face value and the investor receives a rate of return through price appreciation and the bond is redeemed at face value.

Book Value   The value at which an asset is carried on a balance sheet. Normally, the asset is calculated as actual cost less allowances for depreciation. Book value may be more or less than market value.

Broker-Dealer   A firm or individual acting as both a principal and an agent. A broker acts on behalf of the client searching for the best deal in the market place. A dealer acts on behalf of itself in making the market. The dealer actually buys and sells and maintains inventories of securities. A broker carries out the transaction but does not take possession of the security or maintain inventories.

Bull Market   A period of rising prices. The beginning of a bull stock market usually signals economic growth.

Callable Bond   The right of the issuer to call back or redeem a bond at a specified amount at a predetermined time prior to maturity. This is usually done in periods of interest rate declines. The issuer calls the higher interest paying bond and sells a new issue at the lower rates.

Capital   Money used to make money.

Capital Appreciation   An increase in the principal value of an investment.

Capital Depreciation   A decrease in the principal value of an investment.

Capital Gain Distribution   It is the realized gain on the sale of capital assets paid out to the shareholders.

Capital Growth   An increase in the market value of a security over the original purchase price, or an increase in the value of a mutual fund as reflected in the net asset value of the shares.

Certificate of Deposit (CD)   Debt instrument issued by a bank. Most CDs pay interest. The maturities range from 30 days to five years. Interest rates are set by market place competition. It is important to shop around for the best yields.

Chapter 7   Legal term wherein insolvency requires the liquidation of a business entity.

Chapter 11   A court-approved reorganization of a business. The debtor continues to operate the business and allows for negotiation in restructuring and repayment of outstanding debts.

Class of Shares   Shares issued by the same company having different rights or powers. For example Class A shares may be voting shares, while Class B shares are not. In the case of mutual funds, different classes are structured to provide for various forms of sales charges. For example, Class A shares may contain a front-end sales load, whereas Class B shares may contain deferred sales charges along with 12b-1 charges.

Closed-End Investment Company   A management company that operates a mutual fund. A specified number of shares is initially offered, and the shares trade through the public markets. Supply and demand determine the price as with any listed security. These funds are freely tradable. They are sold not redeemed and quoted at current market price not at net asset value.

Commercial Paper Short-term debt obligations with normal maturities ranging from several days to nine months. The debt is usually discounted, issued by banks and corporations, and normally unsecured although often backed by a bank line of credit.

Commingled Fund Pools of money that are established and professionally managed similarly to a mutual fund.

Commodity Any tangible good. Bulk products such as grains and foods are traded on a commodities change.

Common Stock A security representing ownership in a company. Stock holders actually own part of the corporate assets and so share in the profits and losses. Voting shareholders have the right to attend annual meetings and voice opinions on the general operations. Many shareholders have the right to elect the board of directors, and vote on important changes within the organization. Many companies pay annual dividends. Bond holders, on the other hand, are simply creditors with no ownership privileges.

Compound Annual Interest Interest on principal plus previous interest. For example, if you invest $1,000 at 10 percent for five years, you will receive $1,100 at the end of the first year, and that $1,100 is now the basis for the 10 percent interest for the second year and so on. At the end of five years, you have accumulated $1,610.51. If compounding monthly, the total would be $1,645.28. The shorter the compounding period, the greater ending value.

Contingent Deferred Sales Charge (CDSC) A fee often charged when shares are redeemed during the first few years of ownership. Check the prospectus for details.

Contractual Plan A plan designed for periodic fixed dollar investments over a specified period of time such as 10–15 years. A substantial portion of the total sales charge is often deducted in the early periods.

Current Yield Annual dividend or interest rate divided by the current market price.

Custodian Bank or financial institution that actually holds the securities and assets for a client or fund.

Debt-Equity Ratio   Total liabilities divided by total shareholder equity. This ratio gives an indication of how much equity would be available to pay off creditors in a liquidation situation. The higher the ratio, the higher the debt level. For example, a ratio of 3 : 1 indicates that the debt level is three times the value of the equity in the firm.

Defined Benefit Pension Plan   A retirement plan that promises to pay a predetermined amount to an employee who retires after a specified number of years. Some plans permit additional employee contributions, some only permit employer contributions. Separate accounts are not set up for each individual.

Defined Contribution Plan   A retirement plan in which the employer and/or employee contribute specified amounts. A separate account is established for each individual. The ending retirement benefits are determined by the amount of assets accumulated at the time of retirement. The account may be controlled by the firm-appointed trustee or self directed by the employee. Examples: Profit sharing plans, money purchase plans.

Depreciation   The loss in value of an asset. In economic terms it may be due to adverse market conditions. In general business, it may be due to physical damages, obsolescence, or other outside factors.

Derivative   A type of security whose value is derived from an underlying asset. Derivatives range from simple option contracts, to forward and future contracts, to extremely complex and volatile products such as interest rate or currency swaps. Except for the plain vanilla derivatives such as options, these products are better left to the sophisticated institutional traders.

Discount   (1) The difference between a bond's current price and its face value. (2) Some debt instruments such as Treasury bills and zero coupon bonds are sold at prices far below the actual maturity value. With deep discount instruments, there is no interest. With regular debt securities, your total return is comprised of the face value at maturity and annual interest. However, if a bond or bill is deep discounted you only get one payment and that is at time of sale or redemption. The yield is determined by the price appreciation not the interest.

Discount Rate   The interest rate charged by the Federal Reserve for loans to member banks. The Fed changes rates in an attempt to control monetary policy. When the Fed increases rates, or tightens the money supply, entities borrow less, and consequently there is less money available for all uses. The effect is to slow down the economy. The alternative is that the Fed lowers rates, or eases the money supply. Money is more readily available, encouraging economic growth.

Discounted Cash Flow   A method used to estimate the present value of future earnings or cash flows.

Diversification   A method of reducing risk through asset allocation. By investing in several different trading vehicles such as stocks, bonds, real estate, and so on, the risk associated with owning only one asset is spread out. That is, if the stock market drops, the bond market may go up offsetting unrealized stock losses, and so on.

Dividend   The payment designated by the board of directors to be distributed pro rata among the shares outstanding. On preferred shares, it is generally a fixed amount. On common shares, the dividend varies with the fortunes of the company and the amount of cash on hand. It may be omitted if business is poor or the directors determine to withhold earnings to invest in plant and equipment. Sometimes a company will pay a dividend out of past earnings even if it is not currently operating at a profit.

Dividend Payout Ratio   The percentage of earnings paid to shareholders. As a generalization, the higher the ratio the more mature and established the company. Start-up and companies in fast-growing industries usually reinvest all earnings and do not pay dividends.

Dollar-Cost Averaging   A system of buying securities at regular intervals with a fixed dollar amount. Under this system investors buy by the dollars' worth rather than by the number of shares. If each investment is of the same number of dollars, payments buy more shares when the price is low and fewer when it rises. Thus temporary downswings in price benefit investors if they continue periodic purchases in both good times and bad and the price at which the shares are sold is more than their average cost.

Dow Theory   Market analysis based upon the performance of the Dow Jones industrial and transportation stock price averages. The theory says that the market is in a basic upward trend if one of these averages advances above a previous important high, accompanied or followed by a similar advance in the other. When the averages both dip below previous important lows, this is regarded as confirmation of a downward trend.

Dow Jones   A reputable financial information services company. The Dow Jones Industrial Average (DJIA) and the Dow Jones Transportation Average (DJTA) are two of several indexes monitored daily by the financial experts as overall indicators of stock market performance.

Duration   Time weighted life of a bond with the weights being the cash flows. It denotes the years necessary to recover the investment; for example, if the duration is 7.2, that means it will take 7.2 years to recoup the investment.

Earnings Per Share (EPS)   That portion of a company's profits allocated to the shareholders. Primary earnings per share are net income less preferred dividends divided by the weighted average common stock outstanding. For example, if a company earned a profit of $1 million and had 1 million shares outstanding, the reported EPS would be $1 per share.

Earnings Report   A statement—also called an income statement—issued by a company showing its earnings or losses over a given period. The earnings report lists the income earned, expenses, and the net result.

Earnings Yield   The earnings-price ratio. The earnings divided by the current price. It refers to the relationship of EPS to the current stock price.

Economic Growth   The increase in real value of the economy's production of goods and services. Most often expressed as Gross National Product (GNP), or Gross Domestic Product, (GDP).

Employee Retirement Income Security Act (ERISA)   The 1974 law that created the Pension Benefit Guaranty Corporation. ERISA laws established specific guidelines for managing pension funds and eased eligibility regulations.

Employee Stock Ownership Plan (ESOP)   A program that permits employees the opportunity to buy stock in their own company, giving the employees some voice in the firm's management.

Equivalent Taxable Yield   A comparison of the tax-free yield on a municipal bond to that of a corporate bond.

Exchange Privilege   The right of shareholders to switch from one mutual fund to another in the same family of funds, usually at no additional charge. This allows the investor to take advantage of market swings, such as moving money from a conservative money market fund to an aggressive growth fund if the market is believed to be turning more bullish.

Ex-Dividend Date   Date on which the stock trades without the dividend. The stock price is automatically reduced by the dividend amount on the opening. An investor who buys on or after "ex" date is not entitled to the dividend payment.

Family of Funds   A group of various funds sponsored by one issuer. Each fund has its own investment objectives.

Federal Agency Issue   Debt security issued by an agency of the federal government. An example is the Federal National Mortgage Association or more commonly known as Fannie Mae. These securities are not direct obligation of the U.S. Treasury, and as such are not fully guaranteed by the government. However, they are sponsored by federal agencies and usually have high credit ratings.

Federal Deficit   Shortfall created when the federal government spends more in a fiscal year than it receives in revenues. The federal government spending sprees only began to be of national concern within the past 20 years. To cover the continual shortfall, the governments sells long-and short-term debt to the public.

Federal Funds Rate   Interest rate charged by banks with excess reserves at a Federal Reserve district bank to other banks who need overnight loans. The Fed Fund rate is the most sensitive gauge as to the direction of interest rates.

Fiduciary   A person, company, or association who is charged with the responsibility of investing the assets of the beneficiary in a prudent manner. An example is a trustee of a pension fund, or an executor of a will.

Fixed Income Investment   Normally refers to government, municipal, and corporate issues. These securities usually pay a fixed rate of return.

Floater   A debt security with a variable interest rate tied to another interest rate. It provides incremental interest if the pertinent interest rate rises. However, if the consensus is that rates are declining, it is better to buy fixed rate instruments.

Form 10Q   The quarterly financial report filed by every issuer of listed securities. It is filed with the SEC.

Form 10K   The annual audited report required to be filed by the SEC by all registered and/or exchange listed issuers, and all companies with more than 500 shareholders, or $1 million in gross assets.

Forward Contract   An agreement between two parties in which one party is obligated to deliver a stated amount of an asset at a specific time in the future. Forward contracts are drawn up to meet the specific needs of the parties. An example is an agreement between a farmer and a wholesaler for the sale and delivery of a load of grain after harvest. Forwards are not traded on any exchange.

Front-End Load   A sales charge applied to an investment at the time of initial purchase.

Futures Contract   Standardized forms of forward contracts which are securitized and traded on an exchange. It obligates the buyer to purchase the underlying asset at a predetermined time and price. Futures are used for: speculation, hedging, and arbitrage.

Government National Mortgage Association (GNMA)   Also known as Ginnie Mae. It is a government owned agency of HUD which assists in housing financing. It guarantees the full and timely payment of monthly principal and interest on mortgage-backed securities.

Gross Domestic Product (GDP)   Also known as GNP (Gross National Product). It is the total value of goods and services produced in the national economy in a given year. It is the primary indicator of economic growth.

Guaranteed Income Contract (GIC)   A contract between an insurance company and a corporate profit-sharing or pension plan that guarantees a specific rate of return on the invested capital over the life of the contract.

Insider   Directors, officers, and others who know of or have access to confidential information about a firm, which has not been released to the general public. Under the SEC rules, an insider is not permitted to trade the stock on the basis of such information.

Internal Rate of Return (IRR)   A discount rate at which the present value of future cash flows equal the cost of the investment. When the IRR is greater than the required return, the investment presents a good opportunity.

Intrinsic Value   The value of tangible assets or materials. Financial analysts use specific data models on stocks to ascertain whether the "real" current value is consistent with the current market price. If the intrinsic value is greater than the current market price, the stock would be considered undervalued and a buy recommendation.

Investment Advisers Act   Legislation passed by Congress in 1940 that requires all investment advisers to register with the SEC and abide by SEC regulations. It was designed to protect the public against misrepresentation and fraud.

Investment Company   A trust or corporation whose assets are held for investment and are readily marketable. For a management fee, the company invests the pooled money of many investors. The two most common types are open-end mutual funds and closed-end management companies.

Investment Grade   Term used in bond rating. It indicates that the bond is suitable for prudent investors. Fiduciaries often need to maintain credit quality levels and tend to buy mostly investment grade level debt.

Initial Public Offering (IPO)   The issuance of new stock by a corporation. A prospectus must be delivered to each investor before or at the time of sale. A hot new issue is an IPO that is in great public demand. There are not enough new shares to go around. Once the issue is initially priced, the stock usually jumps dramatically in price or sells at a premium to accommodate the demand.

Junk Bond   A debt security with speculative credit rating of BB or lower according to Standard & Poor's or Moody's rating systems. The lower credit rating requires a higher yield.

Leverage   The use of borrowed funds to increase profitability and buying power. In accounting and finance, it is the amount of long-term debt relative to equity. The higher the ratio the greater the leverage.

Leveraged Buyout (LBO)   The takeover of a firm using borrowed capital. Often, the company's assets are used as collateral for the loans.

Liquidity   The ability to convert assets into immediate cash. Short term investments such as money markets and T-bills are considered liquid instruments whereas long-term bonds and stocks are assumed to be less liquid.

Management Fee   The amount charged against investor assets for advisory services. The standard industry mutual fund management fee is approximately 0.5 percent of fund assets.

Margin   The difference between the current market value of the collateral and the amount of the loan. Brokerage margin accounts are governed by Federal Reserve Board Regulation T, which is currently at 50 percent. Brokerage houses charge interest on the borrowed funds. However, it is often less than the cost of bank loans.

Maturity   The date on which a bond's principal is due and repaid to the investor.

Modified Adjusted Gross Income (MAGI)   Adjusted Gross Income (see definition), without taking into consideration the tax deduction for a contribution to a traditional IRA.

Moody's Investor Services   One of the two foremost financial rating agencies. It rates most of the publicly held corporate and municipal bonds and many of the government issues.

Moving Average Chart   A tool used by technical analysts to track stock or commodity price movements. It plots average daily prices for specific periods searching for trends. The actual period continually adjusts as time goes by. That is, as each day passes, the chart drops the earliest day's figures and adds the most recent day's prices.

Municipal Bond   A debt instrument issued by a state or local government. The interest is exempt from federal income taxation, and also exempt from federal and local tax in the issuing state. There are generally two types: General Obligations (GO), and revenue bonds. GOs are backed by the full faith and credit of the taxing power of the issuer and revenue bonds are backed by the particular revenues or incomes from the project.

Mutual Fund   A regulated investment company that pools money and invests in various assets. There are many types such as growth funds, income funds, bond funds, and so on, all designed for a specific objective. Open-end mutual funds are fairly liquid in that investments and redemption transactions occur on a daily basis at net asset value.

National Association of Security Dealers (NASD)   A self-regulatory organization (SRO) operating under the supervision of the SEC. Its purpose is to standardize practices, establish high ethical standards, and enforce fair and equitable rules.

Net Asset Value   Total assets less intangible assets less all liabilities divided by number of shares outstanding. In mutual funds, it is known as the bid price or NAV.

No-Load Fund   A mutual fund operated by an open-end investment company that does not assess a sales charge. Shares are purchased directly from the fund, and not sold through a broker as is normal in a load fund.

Nominal Name   The person in whose name securities are registered if that person is other than the beneficial owner. This is the role of a brokerage firm when securities are registered in street name in an client's account.

Nominal Yield Curve   A chart indicating long-term debt with higher yields than short-term debt.

Open-End Management Company   An investment company that makes mutual fund shares continually available to the public. The mutual fund is the buyer and seller unlike closed-end companies where the securities trade on an exchange and the public is considered to be both buyer and seller.

Operating Expense   The amount paid for asset maintenance or the cost of doing business. Corporate and fund earnings are distributed after deducting for operating expenses.

Portfolio   A group of securities held by an individual or institution which may contain various types of assets such as stocks and bonds. The purpose of a portfolio is to diversify risk. Portfolio managers are professionals responsible for the securities portfolio.

Price Earnings Ratio (P/E)   Stock price divided by last year's earnings. The P/E indicates how much the stock owner pays per dollar of earnings that is generated by the firm on each share. As a generality, the higher the P/E ratio, the more risky and volatile a stock.

Primary Market   The market in which new issues (IPOs) are sold. A market is primary if the proceeds of the sale go to the issuer.

Prime Rate   The interest rate banks charge their most creditworthy customers. The rate is determined by the market forces that affect a bank's cost of funds and the rates that borrowers will accept. The prime rate is a key interest rate for commercial lending.

Prospectus   A document that describes the financial details about a new issue, and is required to be distributed to all investors prior to or at the time of the initial investment. Open-end mutual fund companies must send one to each new investor because the fund continually issues new securities.

Retained Earnings   The net profits reinvested in the business after dividends are paid.

Reinvestment Privilege   The option to have all dividends and capital gains automatically reinvested to purchase more shares. Most funds have this option, as do many listed companies.

Required Rate of Return   For a given level of risk, the return required by investors. If the investor needs an annual return of 10 percent, but the asset only pays 7 percent, the investment would not be a wise choice.

Return of Capital   A distribution that is not paid out of earnings and profits. It is a return of the investor's investment.

Return on Equity (ROE)   Net worth divided by net income. Expressed as a percentage it is an indication of how well the company is using its money.

Risk   The possibility that an investment will not perform as anticipated. An acceptable degree of risk must be determined by the individual with the understanding that the higher the expected return, the greater the risk factor. There are many different kinds of risk, such as exchange, inflation, interest rate, liquidity, political. Most investors are considered to be risk adverse. That is, they seek security over risk.

Sales Charge   Also known as sales load. It is the fee charged on an investment, and varies according to the fund and investment. The charge is added to the net asset value when determining the offering price.

Secondary Market   The exchange or over-the-counter market where shares are traded after the initial offering.

Securities and Exchange Commission (SEC)   The federal agency that regulates and supervises the selling of securities to prevent fraud and unfair practices and to maintain fair and orderly markets.

Selling Short   Selling assets not actually owned. The seller hopes the price will decline and thus makes a profit by buying the securities at a lower price. The risk level is considered to be much higher than buying long and selling when the stock goes up.

Shareholders' Equity   Total assets less total liabilities. Also called net worth.

Soft Dollar Refers to paying a higher commission than could be negotiated for additional services such as research and technology.

Spread The difference between the bid and offer prices. If a stock is quoted at 42–42½, the spread is $.50.

Standard Deviation A statistical measure of a probability distribution. It measures the degree to which a specific value in a probability distribution varies from the expected return or value. The term is often used in portfolio theory where past performance is used in an estimation of possible future performance. The greater the dispersion or deviation, the more risk is involved.

Standard & Poor's Corporation One of the two foremost financial rating agencies. It rates most of the publicly held corporate and municipal bonds and many of the government issues. The company is also noted for its indexes which measure the change in performance of various groups of stocks.

Stock Dividend A dividend paid in additional shares of stock rather than in cash.

Stock Split The division of a company's existing stock into share. In a 2-for-1 split, each stockholder would receive an additional share for each share formerly held.

Stockbroker An agent who for commission handles the public's order to buy and sell securities.

Stop-Limit Order An order placed with a broker to buy or sell at a specified price or better after a given stop price has been reached or passed.

Stop-Loss Limit An order placed with a broker to buy or sell when a certain price is reached, designed to limit an investor's loss on a security position.

Time Horizon The length of time an investment is held.

Total Debt to Total Assets Short-term and long-term debt divided by total assets of the firm. A measure of a companies financial risk that indicates how much of the assets of the firm have been financed by debt.

Trading Range   The spread of prices that a stock normally sells within.

Transaction Costs   Costs incurred buying or selling securities. These include broker's commissions and dealers, spreads (the difference between the price the dealer paid for a security and the price the security can be sold).

Valuation   The process of determining the current worth of an asset.

Variability   The possible different outcomes of an event. An investment with many different levels of return would have great variability.

Warrant   The long-term option that guarantees the right to purchase a stated number of shares of common stock in a company at a specified (exercise) price.

Wilshire 5000 Equity Index   A stock measure comprised of 5,000 equity securities. It includes all New York Stock Exchange and American Stock Exchange issues and the most active over-the-counter issues. The index represents the total dollar value of all 5,000 stocks.

Yield   Also known as return. The dividends or interest paid by a company expressed as a percentage of the current price. A stock with a current market value of $40 a share paying dividends at the rate of $3.20 is said to return 8 percent ($3.20 divided by $40.00). The current yield on a bond is figured the same way.

Yield to Maturity   The yield of a bond to maturity takes into account the price discount from or premium over the face amount. It is greater than the current yield when the bond is selling at a discount and less than the current yield when the bond is selling at a premium.

About the Authors

KNUTE IWASZKO has been a chemist, a salesman, and an innkeeper—and now manages his investment portfolios from the home he shares with his wife at the Jersey shore.

BRIAN O'CONNELL writes on business and personal finance for TheStreet.com, *Financial Planning*, the *Boston Herald*, and *Investor Relations*, among other publications. He has worked with leading financial planner Jonathan Pond on *The New Century Family Money Book*, as well as on articles, newsletters, and television and radio projects. He lives and works in Framingham, Massachusetts.

Printed in the United States
by Baker & Taylor Publisher Services